AFGHAN WOMEN IN TRANSITION

YESTERDAY, TODAY AND TOMORROW

AFGHAN WOMEN IN TRANSITION

YESTERDAY, TODAY AND TOMORROW

ANWESHA GHOSH

University of Calcutta

Centre for Pakistan and West Asian Studies (CPWAS)

Institute of Foreign Policy Studies (IFPS)

in association with

KNOWLEDGE WORLD

KW Publishers Pvt Ltd
New Delhi

University of Calcutta

The Court of Directors of the East India Company sent a despatch in July, 1854 to the Governor-General of India in Council, suggesting the establishment of the Universities of Calcutta, Madras and Bombay. In pursuance of that despatch, the University of Calcutta was founded on January 24, 1857. The University adopted in the first instance, the pattern of the University of London and gradually introduced modifications in its constitution.

The Centre for Pakistan and West Asian Studies, Calcutta University, was set up in 2005 under the UGC Area Studies Programme. It is the only research outfit associated with a University in eastern India with an exclusive focus on Pakistan and West Asian countries, Afghanistan, Iran and Iraq in particular, which together constitute a part of India's extended neighbourhood in the West. The Centre, since its establishment in 2005, has tried to develop a greater understanding of this extended neighbourhood by looking at the internal dynamics of the region with far greater detail than is generally accorded by other area studies outfits in the country.

The Institute of Foreign Policy Studies (IFPS) at the University of Calcutta is an autonomous centre devised for the study of international relations, with particular emphasis on foreign policy. Funded by the Ministry of External Affairs (MEA), Government of India, the institute purports to create a pool of foreign policy specialists capable of offering advice on matters pertaining to India's international relations. The Institute has already been earmarked for developing regional expertise with reference to the Government of India's Look East Policy, and that towards West Asia. The IFPS has also been chosen as one of the ten centres for United Nations Academic Initiative, functioning as the hub for studies on peace and conflict resolution.

ISBN 978-93-86288-55-4 Hardback
ISBN 978-93-86288-56-1 ebook

Published in India by

KNOWLEDGE WORLD

Kalpana Shukla
KW Publishers Pvt Ltd
4676/21, First Floor, Ansari Road
Daryaganj, New Delhi 110002
Phone: +91.11.23263498/43528107
Email: kw@kwpub.com
www.kwpub.com

Printed and Bound in India

CONTENTS

ACKNOWLEDGEMENTS

This project was undertaken as a part of a Visiting Fellowship Program offered by the Centre for Pakistan and West Asian Studies (CPWAS), University of Calcutta in the year 2012. I am grateful to the Centre for its generous support for my field trip to Afghanistan, for conducting this project. A significant part of what this study seeks to address is a product of my counters and interactions with everyday life rhythms of the women (and men) of Afghanistan witnessed during my trip. I owe a special thanks to Dr. Kingshuk Chatterjee, the Deputy Director of CPWAS for his sustained support and encouragement; without his guidance and backing this study would have remained impoverished in more ways than one. I must also thank Dr. Shantanu Chakrabarti and the Institute of Foreign Policy Studies, Kolkata for supporting my project.

I would like to express my deepest gratitude to Dr. Saeed Parto and his colleagues at the Afghanistan Public Policy Research Organization (APPRO) for hosting me and to Mr. Syed Shah of United Nations Assistance Mission in Afghanistan (UNAMA) for introducing me to the organization. The help that I received from Mr. Zalmai Wafamal, First Secretary, the Embassy of the Islamic Republic of Afghanistan in New Delhi was also significant. While in Kabul, each and every member of Afghanistan Research and Evaluation Unit (AREU) extended their unending cooperation and I am indebted to them for that. It was an honour to interact with respected Nancy Hatch Dupree and her team at Afghanistan Centre at Kabul University (ACKU); who gave me complete access to a treasure-trove of rich archival collection. I was really touched by the *mehmannawazi* of my friends Tariq Sapi and Abdullah

Sapi, who were also my translators for some of the interviews. The timely assistance I got from the Embassy of India in Kabul was extremely significant. Last but not the least, my heartfelt thanks go to my parents for their encouragement and love that kept me going; even under trying circumstances.

I owe so very much to so many incredible Afghan women I met, spoke and listened to in and outside Afghanistan, that it is simply not possible to fully spell it out or name them all. My debts to them are immeasurable. I dedicate this book to all those wonderful Afghan women I have met so far and will meet in the future.

GLOSSARY

Al- Amr bi-al-mar.ruf wa-al-nahy an almunkar- the promotion virtue and prevention of vice

Burqa or *chadri*- loose garment completely covering a woman's body and face

Jihad- holy war

Loya Jirga- Grand Assembly

Madrasa- religious school

Mahram- women to be accompanied by their husbands or male blood relatives

Mehr- marriage gift

Meshrano Jirga- Upper House of the Parliament

Mujahideen- fighters of the holy war

Pashtunwali- the customary law of the Pashtuns

Pul- Bridge

Sharia- Islamic Law

Shura- Traditional Afghan decision-making body

Wolesi Jirga- Lower House of the Parliament

Zanane bee Sarparast- unprotected women

ACRONYMS

ACKU	Afghanistan Centre at Kabul University
AIHRC	Afghanistan Independent Human Rights Commission
ANDS	Afghanistan National Development Strategy
APPRO	Afghanistan Public Policy Research Organization
AREU	Afghanistan Research and Evaluation Unit
AWC	Afghan Woman Council
AWN	Afghan Woman Network
CIA	Central Intelligence Agency
DOAW	Democratic Organization for Afghan Women
HAWCA	Humanitarian Assistance for the Women and Children of Afghanistan
IMF	International Monetary Fund
ISAF	International Security Assistance Force
ISI	Inter Service Intelligence Agency
NATO	North Atlantic Treaty Organization
NGO	Non-governmental Organization
NSS	National Security Strategy
PDPA	People's Democratic Party of Afghanistan
PRT	Provincial Reconstruction Team
RAWA	Revolutionary Association of the Women of Afghanistan
UNDP	United Nations Development Program
UNHCR	United Nations High Commissioner for Refugees
UNICEF	United Nations Children's Fund
UNSC	United Nations Security Council
USIP	United States Institute of Peace

INTRODUCTION

I'm the women who has awoken
I've arisen and become a tempest through the ashes of my burnt children
I've arisen from the rivulets of my brother's blood
My nation's wrath has empowered me
My ruined and burnt villages fill me with hatred against the enemy...
Oh compatriot, oh brother, no longer regard me weak and incapable
With all my strength I'm with you on the path of my land's liberation.
My voice has mingled with thousands of arisen women
My fists are clenched with the fists of thousands of compatriots
Along with you I've stepped up to the path of my nation,
To break all these sufferings all these fetters of slavery.
Oh compatriot, oh brother, I'm not what I was
I'm the women who has awoken
I've found my path and will never return.

— Meena Keshwar Kamal[1]

The status of women in Afghanistan has been intimately linked to the processes of state integration throughout the country's history. The advancement of women's rights provided a reliable barometer for the international community to gauge political climate. But in Afghanistan, the evolution of these rights have been interrupted, stressed with episodes of revolutionary transformations and responses. Non-linear patterns of social and political climate have characterised

Afghanistan's development and recurring upheavals have resulted in a marginalised socio-cultural space for women. Ahmed Rashid, writing in 2000, referred to Afghan women as the "vanished gender" to indicate the plight of this oppressed and deprived section of Afghan society during Taliban regime. From such a position, the announcement of the Government of Afghanistan signalling stress on gender equality as one of the most important cross cutting themes in Afghanistan National Development Strategy (ANDS) 2008-2013, and a commitment to measurable improvement in women's economic opportunities and access to and control over productive assets and income, are undoubtedly humongous steps. In fact the brutal oppression of women under the Taliban regime was cited as one of the justifications for US military intervention in 2001. In no other country in recent times have questions of women's rights and gender equity been so clearly in the forefront of nation-building efforts and regime changes as in Afghanistan. After more than eleven years of international intervention, it can be said that, Afghanistan has gone through another decade of upheaval, which has produced a mixed situation of progress and regress.

The growing visibility of women in public spaces at the centre and in the provinces is the cause of delight of some and despair for others. Since international intervention in Afghanistan post 2001, women in unprecedented numbers have sat in decision making positions, yet today acts of violence against female institutions are escalating. Elsewhere domestic violence has driven women to commit suicide or flee their homes despite the certainty of dire consequences. This contradictory being of women in Afghanistan today springs largely from the rapidity with which attitudes towards traditional male/female behaviour norms are changing, while alternatives remain clouded. No doubt, an examination of the dynamics of developments on gender issues in Afghanistan is an important exercise. This study thus attempts to examine and assess the various roles played by Afghan women from the time of Monarchy to the contemporary times.

Afghanistan's history has been marked with decades of war and social unrest. Following the attacks on New York on 11 September 2001, the nation reached a critical juncture as United States of America (USA) (with backing from other powers), used this as a partial justification for the bombing campaign against Afghanistan. This was a war against the evil of terrorism in which either one was with America or against it. Undoubtedly it was an optimistic start. As Northern Alliance backed by United States (US) Special Forces and massive airpower swept through Afghanistan in 7th October 2001 indicating the onset of *Operation Enduring Freedom*, Al Qaeda and its Taliban hosts were not left with many options but to flee to the safe heavens of south and east or over the borders into Pakistan tribal areas in disarray. Afghanistan had to be rescued from itself[2]- was the overall sense. While there remained confusions and questions about the nature of post 9/11 configuration of Afghanistan, the general feel was that of optimism and victory. The people of Afghanistan, after a century of misrule, were in desperate need of a way to govern themselves that will offer some defence against the abuses of power that have marked Afghan history.

After the fall of the Taliban, women were promised peace, security, development, democracy and liberation. US policy makers characterised gender relations in Afghanistan in ways that legitimized their action. [3] An analogy was made between the defeat of Taliban and Al-Qaeda and the liberation of Afghan women. To create a sustainable progress and prevent a backlash from traditional elements, changes in women's roles had to be envisaged with the historico-religious framework of the Afghan culture. This was never meant to be an easy task. A historical overview of the attempts by different regimes to define women's positions and roles in the society and the subsequent responses it generated, amply indicate that. While women in Afghanistan faced several obstacles, there are also, within Afghan history, a number of important precedents of women playing active roles in the private and public sectors, including politics, business, healthcare, education, the media, and the military, among others. However the depiction of women in Afghanistan by international media has largely been that of passive victims waiting for liberalization. *Chadri*- a pleated garment of pastel hues that enveloped women from head to toe, except for a square of open work embroidery over the eyes to provide limited vision, became almost synonymous with Afghan women. Citing the *Chadri* as a symbol, the Western media described Afghan women as among the least liberated on earth.[4]

This was merely not a post Taliban visualization of Afghan women, Nancy Hatch Dupree, writing in 1978 wondered why the foreign observers report that one can wander for hours in the streets of Kabul without seeing the face of a single women while what she, as a long time resident of Afghanistan sees are completely different. Nancy Hatch Dupree writes:

> "Every weekday morning in Afghanistan's capital, Kabul, scores of women on their way to work stream out of the old city, the middle-class housing developments, and mud walled villages on the outskirts. Teachers, university professors, engineers, doctors and nurses, policewomen,

> factory worker, saleswomen, social workers, actresses, and a number of other working women, they are dressed in the latest fashions. This year it is pants suits and jeans: a few years ago mini-skirts and knee-high boots were in."[5]

Dupree looked at this tendency from the angle of 'cultural bias' and argued that what was present and ignored was noteworthy sign of liberation and what was present and observed was misinterpreted.[6] As discussed in the following chapters, the Afghan history was marked with phases where modernization drives were carried out by state authorities. But an overall review into the matter would indicate that gender policies have always been part of a larger ideological debate between traditionalist and modernist forces in Afghanistan. Efforts to support and emancipate women have often been led by male political leaders as a component of the state's modernization policies. Such gender measures have been challenged repeatedly and at times reversed by the conservative orthodoxy, often composed of religious leaders and the rural population.[7] This pattern has been repeated throughout recent Afghan history, beginning with King Amanullah (1919-1929), continuing with the reign of King Zahir Shah (1933-1973); Daoud's presidency after the coup d'etat (1973-1978); the Marxist regime (1978-1989); the Mujahideen resistance movement (1979-1994); and the Taliban regime (1994-2001). Each of these political movements resulted in a re-evaluation of women's roles, whereby sometimes the legislative reforms tended to support women emancipation while in some other instance they severely curbed women presence in the public space. Although these regimes have been transitory, they have left their influence on Afghan culture.

In the past decade, with the support of international

community Afghan women have catalyzed changes in many sectors although their overall conditions remain difficult. They have taken great personal risks to renegotiate the rigid gender roles and identities imposed upon them by tradition. Since 1979, generations of Afghan women have lived in a country torn by war and have been subjected to subjugation, violence, killing, imprisonment and deprivation. Needless to say, the quest for equal rights for women was never meant to be an easy process. In fact for much of the population, living in rural areas, the question of female employment and education has hardly been an issue. They have worked in land and have been provided with minimal level of education consistent with the role they played. In the urban centres, on the other hand, even in the late twentieth century, it has been the tradition that girls received a reasonable of education, but a married woman generally did not work for living.[8] Therefore like most countries, there has remained a divergence, both at the level of aspiration and experience, among the women from rural and urban Afghanistan. An important aim of this research would be to identify the distinction between the experiences of urban and rural in Afghanistan. However, before focusing at the plight of Afghan women across contexts and periods, it would be important to briefly discuss certain general aspects about Afghanistan and its people.

Land the People of Afghanistan

The modern Islamic Republic of Afghanistan *(Jomhuri-ye Eslami-ye Afghanistan)* is one of the most under developed countries located at a very significant geo-strategic position, at the cross roads of a region which has invited contests between neighbours- the Central Asian Republic to the north, China and India to the east, Pakistan to the south and Iran to the west. This lucrative location of Afghanistan and the porous borders have attracted foreign invaders in the form of Arabs, Iranians, Turks and Mongols. The country's landscape has steep mountain ranges and, deep and narrow valleys that separate and sometimes isolate regions inhabited by people of various cultural backgrounds and lifestyles. Geography has led to the perpetuation of tribalism, regionalism and ethnocentrism.[9] Jan Goodwin calls Afghanistan a country of savage beauty. Its mountains are somewhat highest in the world , while the landscape is harsh, tree and streams dot the terrain.[10] The lack of a modern transportation system, combined with rugged terrain and widespread illiteracy, have inhibited interaction among the diverse ethno-linguistic communities, causing people to rely on their own meagre resources for survival and instilling suspicion for their neighbours.[11] The country's economy is based on subsistence agriculture, with wheat constituting the staple diet. The primary occupation of the people is farming and animal husbandry. There is around 12.13 percent of arable land (as of 2005) and irrigated land of about 27, 200 square kilometres (as of 2003).[12] The farmers generally use primitive instruments for agriculture. Tribal chiefs and feudal landlords posses large stretches of land and poor farmers generally work on small plot of their own land or as tenant farmers for feudal or absentee landlords. Until recently, Afghanistan was the largest producer of poppy. Despite regular clampdowns on opium production and trafficking, Afghanistan's farmers are being forced by poverty to revive the industry. Today the country is one of the poorest countries of the world, because of years of political instability and war that has ruined the economy. Afghanistan has 15 million strong labour force, of which 80% are into agriculture and 20% in industry and services.[13] Years of armed conflict have damaged and destroyed many irrigation systems over the years impacting on the agricultural output. The lack of adequate land to sustain families and civil strife have caused many families to migrate to urban centres in search of employment. Commerce and trade suffered serious setback during the civil war and are currently in a process of slow recovery.[14]

Tribal chiefs and feudal lords known by the titles *Mir, Khan, Malik* and so on are at the top range of the social ladder and wield considerable socio-economic influence. Religious leaders known by the titles *Pir, Shah* belong to upper class families and play a critical role in people's social lives, defending private ownership of property and its corresponding culture, politics and tradition, and persuading illiterate and unworthy people to submit to their leadership, according to Hafizullah Emadi.[15]

Like its geography, the people of Afghanistan are diverse in their ethnicity. The principle ethnic groups of Afghanistan are Pashtun, Uzbek, Tajik, Hazara, Kyrgyz, Baloch, Tarar, Brahui, Turkmen, Nuristani, Kohistani, Pashai, Gujar, Arab, and others. Among them only a few are of indigenous origin and majority are transnational. Hindus and Sikhs, who migrated to Afghanistan from Indian subcontinent, are also a part of Afghanistan's cultural mosaic. Louis Dupree has classified the Afghan into three 'physical types', namely, Caucasoid (mainly Pashtun, Tajik, Baluch, Niristani), Mongoloid (mainly Hazara, Aimak, Turkomans, Uzbeks, Kyrgyz) and modified Australoid (Brahui).[16] There are an estimated forty languages spoken throughout the country, with Dari or Persian as dominant languages, being widely spoken and understood by an overwhelming majority ethnic communities throughout the country. Afghanistan's constitution recognises all spoken languages, however Persian and Pashtu are the two officially recognized languages of the state.[17] The vast majority of the country's population are Muslim, while there are a small number of non-Muslim such as Hindus, Sikhs and Christians. Religion has undoubtedly played a pivotal role in shaping the country's history and civilization from the emergence of Zoroastrianism to Buddhism and Islam.[18] Since Islam is a pluralistic faith, various Islamic practices exist and accordingly Sunni, Shia and Kharijite factions can be found in Afghanistan. An overwhelming 90 percent of the population however follow Sunni Islam, which in combination with local customs and tribal influences; often lead to variations in practices.

The Sunni Pashtuns ruled in Afghanistan since 1747, when the Abdali tribes headed by Ahmed Shah Abdali seized power and laid foundation of Pashtun domination of the country's politics. Struggles for power among rulers caused them to form alliances with imperial power to defend their rule by receiving financial, political and military support to subdue their adversaries and in the process followed the policy of divide and conquer and pitted one ethno religious group against the other in order to maintain their supremacy. Western powers because of the lucrative location were willing to provide this kind of support to maintain their control of the buffer zone. Afghanistan is often dubbed as the "crossroad of empires". Stephen Tanner[19] in his book has toned that the country found itself at the hinge of imperial ambitions since the beginning of recorded history. The borders of today's Afghanistan were mainly drawn out of political and military consideration by the superpowers of those days which were world's greatest sea-faring empire Great Britain and the largest land power Russia. The British and the Russian Boundary Commissions pegged out Afghan borders neither along clear geographical feature, nor on the basis of long accepted historical tradition or ethnic factors.[20] As a result ethnic problems still plague Afghanistan. One of the most prominent blunders was to cut straight through the traditional tribal land of the Pashtuns by Durrand Line (the international border between Pakistan and Afghanistan, which the later do not accept) in 1893. One early British emissary noted that Afghans didn't even have a name for their country, but near the end of the nineteenth century Amir Abdur Rehman Khan began to refer to it as "Yaghistan", a name variously translated as "Land of free" of "Land of rebels". [21]The "Great Game", as the European imperial period was called, took place from 1826 to 1919. Britain and Russia, in the nineteenth century fought for the control of the buffer land of the Afghans. Following that, the previous century was witness to the most gruesome battle fought over Afghanistan between Cold War Rivals, the USA and the USSR- the repercussion of which continue to beleaguer the country even today.[22]

Afghanistan was a monarchy from 1747 up to 1973 although the legitimacy of the state has always been somewhat shaky. Since 1919 a conflict between conservative and modernist Afghan factions gained momentum in the country. Another very important aspect about Afghan political history has been the significant influence of the neighbouring countries on the political dispensations in Kabul while the ordinary Afghans have had little opportunity to participate in the decision- making process that have affected their lives.[23] The tension between the traditionalist and the urban elites influenced by modern ideas reappeared during the communist period between 1978 and 1992. The urban elites had access to education and concepts of society that transcended both the village based hierarchies and those of the Islamic clergy, leading to growing tension between traditionalists and modernizers.[24] As the government started imposing socialist programs, tension started building up in Afghanistan. It was also a time when USA had emerged as the new ascendant superpower after the Second World War. The superpower rivalry that was witness in the previous century between Russia and Britain was duplicated once more this time between an expansionist USSR looking south and the USA looking north from Pakistan, keen to shape developments in Iran, China and Central Asia. Afghanistan drew considerable world attention as Soviet Union became entangled in a conflict between Marxist regime of the People's Democracy Party of Afghanistan (PDPA) and the USA and Saudi Arabia aided and Pakistan trained Islamist rebel forces, the *Muajahideen.* Along with competition, Cold War also brought foreign aid from western sources as well as from Soviet Union.

However, the Soviet armed intervention with its international dimensions had major adverse impact on the country's already fragile state structure and accused immense damage to country's infrastructure. The involvement of international actors like USA, Saudi Arabia and Pakistan to combat the Soviet 'threat' created arms network and an economy that thrived on flourishing drug network, smuggling racket and was left with no indigenous source of revenue. Once Soviet left, civil war gripped the country. The Soviet intervention and the subsequent period of conflict in the country resulted in displacing millions of people and forcing them to live as refugees in neighbouring countries. The intelligentsia and other affluent section of the population whoever could move out shifted to Western nations as refugees or asylum seekers creating a major vacuum of human resource. The institutions that were left continued to disintegrate creating an emptiness there as well. It was into this vacuum that the Taliban emerged towards the end of 1994, as the conflict mutated still further, with factions becoming proxies for the interests of their own regional power sponsors, namely USA, Pakistan, Saudi Arabia on one hand and Iran, Russia, India and Central Asian Republics of Uzbekistan and Tajikistan on the other. The Taliban, covertly supported by Pakistan's powerful Inter-Services-Intelligence Agency, were well armed and had the support of a population disgusted with the behaviour of local warlords. These fighters were largely drawn from Pashtun youths who had spent most of their lives in refugee camps of Pakistan. The Taliban movement was seen as a way of reasserting Pashtun power, to counter the Tajik, Uzbek, Hazara forces who had gained prominence prior to their advent. Most international scrutiny of the Taliban has focused on their particular interpretation of Sharia Law and their treatment of women.

The Taliban's assurance of bringing peace into the war ravaged country failed to hold promise when conflict continued as resistance forces encountered the extremist, radical and primarily Pashtun forces to dominate the country.[25] By mid 2001, the Taliban controlled more than 90% of Afghanistan and the overall situation in the areas they controlled was one of relative peace, in the sense that factional fighting had ceased. However, though they succeeded in establishing a *defacto* government, they were never recognized by international community (except Pakistan, UAE and Saudi Arabia) and their draconian policies, especially pertaining to women earned them severe criticism across the world.

It was during this time that Afghanistan had become the base for Al Qaeda network. Foreign nationals from Arab countries as well as Pakistan and Pakistan occupied Kashmir were trained in Afghan soil (in training camps run by Al Qaeda) to undertake jihad in other parts of the world. This situation first came in prominence in 1998 after the terrorist attacks on US Embassy in Kenya and Dar es Salaam. But the event of

11 September 2001, resulted in the total destruction of World Trade Centre in New York, partial destruction of Pentagon and death of thousands of people, was of an altogether different scale and significance. The destruction was immediately attributed to Al Qaeda and the refusal of Taliban to handover the Al Qaeda leadership, a military campaign aimed at the overthrow of Taliban regime, with the support of the Northern Alliance commenced on October 7, 2001. Their fall from power after the initiation of *Operation Enduring Freedom* paved way for the interim government under Hamid Karzai. Even after more than a decade of international intervention, Afghanistan continues to be plagued by threats of various forms and one of the most significant being the issues pertaining to half of the population of the country- the women of Afghanistan.

Afghanistan is a patriarchal society where kinship plays a prominent role in mobilizing public support and developing alliance. Polygamy has been a common practice among affluent rural and urban families. It has been observed that such practices also help wealthy men to expand their social networks and power by creating alliance. Sons are the sole inheritor of movable and immovable property after the death of the father. Women have been regarded as private property and men are bound to defend and protect their women from strangers, even as they feel entitled to abuse and mistreat women writes Hafisulla Emadi.[26] According to eminent Pakistani author Ahmed Rashid Afghan man's honour is maintained by constant feuding revolving around *zar* (gold), *zan* (woman) and *zamin* (land).[27] The fear of social debacle often seeps through casual observation of Afghan culture, like a remark from the 1962 study by a group of American scholars: "Water ranks with property and women as a source of dispute in Afghanistan."[28] The rise of Islamic orthodoxy and orthopraxy since 1980s has forced women to cover their bodies from head to toe in bulky garments; Islamists maintain that seclusion of women are based on Islamic ethos, while modernist liberals and progressives disagree with such rationalization. The identity of Afghan women is multidimensional and imbedded in special factors such as their extended family network, ethnicity (Hazara, Uzbek, Pashtun, etc), religion (Sunni, Shiite), language (Pashto, Farsi, Tajiki, Dari), social class (based on sharp socio-economic divides), urban/rural background, education, and political affiliation. Afghan women's situations and needs vary according to these factors.

Afghanistan has always been a conservative society with traditional values and strong religious beliefs. While Islam was a unifying force among different regional identities and groups, religious practice was one of choice and often observed with tolerance and respect. However in thirty years of political upheavals and war, this attitude of tolerance has diminished; there has been a radicalization of Afghan culture, affecting both religious practice and attitudes towards gender. This situation developed during the Soviet intervention continued throughout the time the Mujahideen were in control, and became even more extreme during the Taliban period. Over the past few decades the spread of Islamic fundamentalism has created a pan-Islamic culture that exerts itself through state control. This powerful state ideology has been further intensified by the Western response to 9/11 further strengthened the anti-western ideology leading to deeper Islamization of Middle East and Asia.[29] Decades of religious conservatism have left a mark on Afghan society. Helen Hardacre points out that, "Religion as a cultural force in human history has been remarkably powerful in establishing long lasting, influential motifs of gender...Religions invest the family with sacred significance, and this extends to gender and interpersonal relations. The family is the primary unit for ritual observance as well as an influential site of religious education and the transmission of religious knowledge from one generation to the next."[30] Given the present condition of life in Afghanistan, religion may be perceived as the only force able to reinstate a sense of nationhood, kinship solidarity and economic and political empowerment against what are seen as corrupting western ideologies and forces. As in the past, Afghan leaders continue to build their support of women on the foundation of Islam. Thus, it would be interesting to understand the complex relationship between gender and Islam, particularly in reference to Afghanistan.

Islam and Gender: A Complex Relationship

According to Louis Dupree, early Islam, did not consider women inferior and they played active political, social and economic roles. Yet for centuries, the customs of purdah, the isolation of women from all men except male relations have been justified as a religious sanction. Dupree maintained that a careful examination of Koran, the Hadith and the Hanafi Sharia's of Sunni Islam, "reveals no definite, unqualified requirement for purdah and the veil." He noted that the dress code was not practiced by rural women who worked in the fields.[31] As a patriarchal agrarian society it created a legacy of distinct gender roles and "...tribal traditions where men exercise unmitigated power over women.[32] The structure of Afghan societies—especially in rural areas—are based around strong tribal and ethnic divisions with honor systems playing a major role in the various groups' customs and their attitudes towards women. These honor codes center primarily around the preservation of their purity and morality. Women are used as pawns that help create and seal alliances between tribes through marriages, which are usually planned without the consent of the brides. In these unions, "...total obedience to the husband and his family is expected, and women are prevented from getting any education."[33] Emmanuel Todd wrote that Islam is formulated in "vague, general and moralizing language." The Muslim women is protected in theory and in practice in the sense that the Koran, as a doctrine, seeks to improve a woman's position and her marriage, psychologically, within a specific tribe or similar social unit, but "protection is not equality."[34] The tribal system is basically "embodied in separation of sexes." He argued that the cultural price paid for the social elimination of women is the retardation of education and long term social stagnation.[35]

Zeiba Shorish-Shamley says that Islam, in theory, gave men and women equal rights in every aspect of life: marriage, creation, spiritual status, education, work, owning property, having wealth, being able to inherit, and the right to live. Islamic law forbids forced marriages. In addition, the Koran grants a woman the right to won her *mahr*, which is the payment that the husband makes to the wife as a part of marriage contract in relations to divorce. She has equal rights to divorce.[36] Shamley points at Sura2, Verse 228, "...women shall have rights similar to rights against them, according to what is equitable. But men have a degree (of advantage) over them. And Allah is Exalted in Power, Wise."[37] Some see the degree as a degree of intelligence, others, superiority; and others, relevant to maintenance of the family in that degree is based in economics.[38] Sura 4, Verse 3 addresses the marriage of a man to two to four women in order to deal justly with orphans and war widows. In verse 129, the Koran states that a man is not capable of treating all wives equally and justly in every respect of life. Shorish-Shamley thus interpreted it as "in truth, Islam encourages marriage with only one women."[39] However several Afghan men and women interviewed in the course of this research expressed almost unanimously that Islam permits men to have up to four wives. While men expressed that they did not see anything unjustified in marrying more than ones in circumstances where the wife unable to give birth to his child or is "incapable to make him happy."[40] Women on the other hand felt that since the religion has given men this privilege, "it is quite natural that they would like to exercise it."[41] Shamley however believes that Islam doesn't encourage marriage with one women. Shura 4, Verse 11 states, "Allah (thus) directs you as regards your children's (inheritance): to the male, a portion equal to that of two females..."[42]. Some argue this verse does not benefit females economically while others say it is fair because a man is legally obligated to "maintain" his wife, children, parents and other relatives in need and a woman doesn't have any such obligations.

Professor Abdul Raheem Yasser[43] spoke from the experience about how the Afghan women have been looked upon: "Women are very much esteemed. They are important members of the family and religiously they are put in a very high position. Our books and beliefs have taught us that paradise is at the foot of the mother and if anybody other than God deserves to be worshipped, it is the mother; and it is the mother that forms the life of her family and she is the centre and the focal point of attention and respect."He however, admitted that women's freedom varies in different situation and spaces and gave a comparison of women in Afghanistan and America and said that their freedoms would obviously vary.

While central to the heritage of Afghanistan and other

countries that have a history of repressive gender policies, Islam is not necessarily the force that has led to women's subordination believes a section of Afghan population today. Within the context of colonialism and the ascendancy of Western norms, a politicized version of Islam has emerged, entailing a rejection of Western culture in favor of an "authentic," more "spiritual" and "pure" way of life. This political movement has often focused on "emancipated women" as a symbol of Westernization and as a threat to the integrity of Islamic and indigenous traditions. With this rationale, laws unfavourable to women have been passed in the name of Islam. Some theologians maintain that Islam is an inherently balanced space, enjoining men and women to be actively involved in social, political, and educational realms to fulfill their religious duties. Those advocating reform of practices within Islam argue that the faith and way of life of the Prophet and his first community should be prioritized over the influences of the internationalization of Islam. This school of thought proposes that the value system of Islam requires *ijtihad*—individual reasoning—to best suit individual and community needs.[45]

There are others who argue that the discourse on women should be removed beyond the realm where religious leaders and the Ulema have the clear advantage. They advocate social change through secular means such as legislation. Many countries in the Muslim world have Shariah (Islamic law) alongside constitutional law to accommodate religious values and current social needs. Often one of the stipulations is that the laws cannot be in violation of the basic principles of Islam. Still others insist that in many parts of the Islamic world, legislation based on religious argument may be best countered by understanding the source of the argument and offering an equal or more powerful religious source for an alternative position.[46] For Muslim women to progress and overcome repressive social structures and legislation within their societies, the first step is often developing an understanding of their rights within the context of Islamic tradition.

Once looked from a historical perspective it can be seen that Islam expanded rapidly, not allowing new converts time to become educated. Thus acculturation and Islamic education of the converts were unsynchronized. Growing wealth and new modes produced a fear for the chastity of its women, and the result was a deterioration of the Muslim women's position status and role.[47] Shorish-Shamley observed, "It is not the Islamic ideologies that determine the position of women in the Islamic societies, it is rather the pre-Islamic patriarchal ideologies existing in a particular society, combined with the lack of education and ignorance that constructed the Muslim women's position."[48]

The Pashtuns, the largest ethnic group in Afghanistan, have a complex honor-based society that exemplifies the way tribal traditions have continued to define women's roles today. *Pashtunwali*, translated literally as "the way of the Pashtuns" is the foundation of this people's identity. Violation of any of the various stipulations prescribed by the code places the defier at risk of being shunned by his or her tribe, making adherence the obvious choice. The *izzat*, or honor of the Pashtun individual, is crucial to their membership in the group—without it, "…he or she is no longer considered a Pashtun, and is not given the rights, protection, and support of the Pashtun community".[49] Members of self-sustaining agrarian communities are interdependent, eliminating exile as an option for survival.

The most important pillar of this extensive system is the purdah, often referred to as the symbolic veil separating the men's sphere from the women's sphere—a segregation necessary to uphold honor. In agrarian societies of Afghanistan, this is often practiced through the division of labor based on gender. Women have been left to care for the household while the men were out shepherding the flocks for days and weeks. Women were expected to remain within their respective sphere and it was common knowledge that consequences arise when these boundaries were crossed. For women, these consequences include getting beaten, accused of dishonour, and even perhaps expelled from the community. There have been thousands of instances when they have been killed in the name of honor. The *purdah* and *izzat* have been most crucial to the survival of the Afghan system of patriarchy because the honor of the male head of a family has been directly dependent on his wife's virtue. In fact, "it is often said that Pashtun men customarily see women as comprising the essence of the family. If a woman earns a bad reputation, her whole family, which includes the men, is sullied".[50] Places where mixing of unmarried or unrelated members of the opposite sex were prevalent, were regarded as areas where moral defilement was likely to occur—unfortunately these places also included schools and hospitals. This explains why such drastic measures were taken to separate the women of Afghanistan from anything that may bring shame to their families—even if it came at the expense of their basic human rights. Though many may confuse the tribal traditions practiced in Islamic countries with the religion of Islam, it is important to note that, though the Pashtuns were Sunni Muslims of the Hanafi school of law, it was their Pashtun tribal code, *Pashtunwali,* which governed them before all else.[51] Afghan society has been structured around tribal divisions and although its people are practicing Muslims, the religion is ordained through tribal leaders who rarely recognize the line that lies between cultural customs and Islamic laws. They conveniently fail to enforce parts of the religion that could potentially obstruct the continuity of their patriarchal system, and the steps they take to preserve their ways are often in clear violation of not only Islam, but also the universal standards of human rights.

The fact that the first word of the Quran revealed was *iqra*, which translates to the command, "read" or "learn" in Arabic, is proof enough of the impact that Islam places on the education of its followers. However, there are numerous other places within the scripture and also in the *hadiths* (words or deeds of the Prophet) in which the education of both males and females is emphasized. The Prophet used to say, for example, that, "education is obligatory on both Muslim men and women, even if they have to go to China to seek it".[52] The reiteration of the importance of learning in Islam is in clear opposition to practices of Taliban era in Afghanistan—a group deeply entrenched in ancient tribal practices. As of 2009, more than 630 schools have been shut down by the Taliban because they have been deemed "un-Islamic".[53] More than 120 school girls and teachers faced poison attack in north Afghanistan in 2012 as the resurgent Taliban was pressing ahead with its campaign to close girls schools ahead of the withdrawal of US and NATO forces in 2014.[54] Ironically, it is the closing down of these educational institutions that are against the tenets of Islam and in comparison, the tribal traditions they have carried throughout the years that condone such actions. With respect to the forced marriages and subservience to men that is expected of women in Afghan tribes, these actions were also condemned in Islam where, "no one – not even her father can force her to marry against her expressed consent. And a woman does not cease to be an individual after marriage".[55]A woman's humanity and singularity is acknowledged in Islam and she is not regarded as property to be beaten and abused as is the case in patriarchal Afghan societies. Tribal leaders abuse their absolute power and, by labelling cultural traditions as religious, they manage to maintain their sexist system of hierarchy.

William Maley pointed out that Koran has a "powerful warning against missionary utopianism" in that it commands there "shall be no compulsion in religion".[56] Hassan Hathout, director of outreach at the Islamic Centre of Southern California, believed that the Taliban knew that the Prophet said, "The pursuit of knowledge is obligatory over every Muslim, male or female." He added that the whole of medical corps of the Prophet's army was an all-women corps, and interesting enough this was happening much before the Western women were legally allowed to serve as soldiers. In some battles Muslim "women took sword and shield and joined active combat, to be later praised by the Prophet.[57] Caliph Omar, the second successor to the Prophet as head of state, appointed a women judge, Al-Shaffa, over commercial affairs. When Omar gave directives regarding the marriage dowry, a woman in the mosque corrected him by citing the Koran. Omar responded, "The women is right and I am wrong."[58] Handout concluded his article by saying "Men and women are equal and obligations (and prohibitions) of Islam apply to them equally."[59]

Organizations like the Muslim Women's League added its voice to these philosophies and argue, "Taliban's stand on the seclusion of women was not derived from Islam, but rather, from a cultural bias found in suppressive movements throughout the region".[60] The organization of Women Living Under Muslim Laws (WLUML), which works in Afghanistan and Pakistan believe that violence always existed in Afghanistan but escalated during the times of conflict and war. The anonymous group believes that women have not come a long way from the time when they were treated worse than livestock.[61] With international intervention hope was raised that situation will change for the women. On November 2002, the new Hamid Karzai government announced the women will be released from prison because the facilities did not meet international standards. Some of the women released were imprisoned for "violation of Sharia laws." However, in provinces like Herat, Taliban like practices of gender segregation and implementation of stringent laws in the name of Islam has returned once America's war ended. By 2003, orders from the chief justice started coming in favour of closure of five cable television stations in Kabul and insisted on an end of coeducation for girls and boys.[62]

According to the UN Universal Standards of Human Rights, the institutionalized patriarchies of Afghan societies violate several articles, including the document's core premise that "...the advent of a world in which human beings shall enjoy freedom of speech and belief and freedom from fear and want has been proclaimed as the highest aspiration of the common people."[63] Women in Afghanistan have been living in the constant fear that they will bring shame upon their families. They live their lives in fear that they will be punished for simply desiring access to an education or healthcare in a public place alongside their fellow human beings. Afghanistan's tribal rituals, as demonstrated by the *Pashtunwali*, were also in clear violation of Article 16 of the Universal Standards, which declares that only marriage between two consenting spouses is humanely permissible.[64] In addition to its transgression of many other standards, the Afghan tradition of segregation—often depriving women of an education altogether—breaches Article 26, which ultimately acknowledges that all human beings have the right to an education.

Objective of this Study

This study is essentially about the women of a country which has seen instability, unrest and violence as a result of decades of war. A culture that advocates the principle of "Men first". A "weak buffer state" of little significance except as a no-man's land between major players in the global political game- rather like the mangled calf carcass that powerful housemen struggle to possess in the Afghan sport of *Buzkashi*. In Afghanistan women have long been portrayed as passive victims. The society created by the Taliban constantly evoked indignation and response of shock and disbelief in the Western press. *Burqa* became synonymous with Afghan women as international press carried picture of *Burqa* clad Afghan women and the symbol of oppression. When the fact is Afghanistan has had elite and middle class women who asserted their rights and marched towards modernization. Conquering injustices from within has always been part of Afghan women's legacy, unfortunately those aspects did not get adequate attention.

This study considers the transition in the position of women in Afghan society under various state authorities starting from the Monarchy up to the current phase of government. The impacts upon women of war and of various regimes of the last few decades; the distinction between the lives of the urban and rural women, women as a work force, marriage practices, population displacement- both internal and external, refugee experiences and different coping up strategies by the population have been dealt with. The developments of the past decades have impacted all possible spheres of Afghan existence, specifically gender. After more than eleven years of international intervention, it can be said that, Afghanistan has gone through another decade of upheaval, which has produced a mixed situation of progress and regress. An attempt has been made to review the position of Afghan women since the beginning of twentieth century which marked a new phase in the story of their survival. As in the past, Afghan women have used different initiatives to make alliances at various levels of society to achieve their goals and defend their gains, which have been reviewed in this study. The study aspires to raise a few fundamental questions: Has there been any significant change in the plight of Afghan women? Was there any genuine attempt to hear their voices in various spheres of personal and public life? Do the women's right exist mostly on paper in Afghanistan? Can the women ever become a powerful force and an important resource in Afghanistan's future? Considering there is a visible resurgence of fundamentalist and conservative elements in Afghan society, the apprehension about Afghan women with regard to their future are justified. Finally an attempt has been made to identify women's voices in contemporary Afghanistan, their achievements, their fears, their apprehensions and understand what expectations women have from Afghan society, nation actors and international supporters in the post 2014 period.

Methodology and Limitation of the Study

First half of this book is a historical survey of the position of women in Afghanistan from Monarchy to the Taliban period. It reviews the different experiences they have under gone with different regimes and their changing attitude and take on women's emancipation in the country. This part of the research was drawn from a variety of source materials ranging from published academic works (books, articles, news paper reports and journals) to journalistic dispatches, folklore, reports of human rights organizations and policy papers. Documentary films on Afghan women available on YouTube have also been referred to for the study. The later half of the research, looks at the more contemporary phase that is, the experiences of the women of Afghanistan since the fall of Taliban regime in Afghanistan. Significant works have been done on gender in respect to Afghanistan since the time of Taliban. The post Taliban phase marked a continuation of academic interest on the subject and subsequently several researches, evaluation studies, policy papers, recommendations have been forwarded by several international and research organizations around the world. This research has been drawn from such sources apart from primary sources.

This is primarily a qualitative study. To achieve the mentioned objectives, semi-structured research schedules were utilized for collecting data from the study Universe. In depth interviews were the primary technique to obtain qualitative data. An important aspect of this research was the attempt to generated responses from both Afghan women and men, residing not only in Afghanistan but around the world. Questionnaire was particularly designed to generate their responses on various pertinent aspects, such as political, social and economic indicators of women. It also tried to capture the opinion of respondents on various issues pertaining to women in Afghanistan. In addition to formal interviews, group discussions, informal conversations with individuals and groups, telephonic interviews, communication via various social network sites were conducted to gather responses from Afghans. Apart from responses of women, this study also intended to take into account the opinion of Afghan men on issues pertaining to their counterpart. The study has extensively draw upon the researcher's experience of interacting with Afghan nationals in various cities of India over a period of past two years and most importantly of the field trips to Kabul, Afghanistan in April 2012. That experience provided an unusual window, especially in exploring the role of memory and history in a context largely defined by oral tradition.

It would not be out of place to add a few words on the data source and the constraints of the research. The opportunity to interact with various Afghan women during the field trip to Kabul, Afghanistan in April 2012, shaped my thinking on the subject. Before the trip gender for me was simply one of the many issues of importance of a country which had fascinated me enough to take it up as my area of research. However, during my interactions with Afghan women, Kabuli women to be specific; who were the representatives of the most empowered and progressive segments (such as educated and skilled professionals) of the society; I realised that even after decades of international intervention and so called 'progress' on paper, a large section of these women feel deprived, alienated and subjugated by patriarchy. The deteriorating security situation, the evaporating international interest and commitment further add to their insecurities. If this was the condition of the relatively privileged section of the country, one could only imagine what the plight of the woman without access to opportunities might be. However, it doesn't mean that the entire encounter was dark and gloomy. The growing visibility of women in public spaces at centre was undoubtedly a huge progress considering their limited scope in the Taliban era. Women are courageous and are determined to break all odds. Despite obstructions, their commitment and perseverance to take their movement forward towards their goals were inspiring. This study has been extremely close to my heart and would not have been possible without my interactions with Afghan women, both in and outside Afghanistan. The situation in Afghanistan did not allow extensive field work across the length and breadth of the country. Therefore information were generated through the process of interviews with Afghans (both men and women) working at academic Institutes like the Afghan Research and Evaluation Unit (ARUE) and Afghanistan Centre at Kabul University (ACKU), interactions with young girls from different departments in Kabul University gave an idea about what they were thinking. Interactions with members of Ministry of Women's Affairs and the women working at *Bagh-e-Zanana* (Women's garden) in Kabul, parliamentarians, media persons, young professionals provided significant inputs to my understanding of situation of women in the country. These interactions also made me realise the distinction between the experiences of Afghan women in the rural areas and the necessity to look beyond Kabul. However, since trips to the provinces were not possible, the information about the rural women were gathered from secondary literature and from the rural experience of Afghan women who are currently in Kabul. Since women are generally accompanied by men, their responses tended to be influenced by the presence of men around them. Though the knowledge of Hindustani and Urdu have been extremely advantageous for interactions, but the dependence on a male interpreter to communicate with elderly women on the streets of Kabul had its own limitation. Lack of first hand information from the provinces, along with many other, remained crippling constraint for this research. Lastly, majority of the responses came from Afghans who were conversant with the English Language; which itself is indicative of the limited reach of this study.

Chapterization

First chapter of the book, attempts to offer a historical overview of the position of women in Afghanistan. It starts evaluation of their position during the time of modern monarchies and in the process focus particularly at two eras that tried to bring space emancipation of women of the country. This chapter ends with the experiences of women during the Taliban period.

Second chapter looks into the differences between the experiences of Afghan women in urban and rural settings. A vast segment of Afghan women live in the provinces, whose concerns, aspirations and priorities have been starkly different from their urban counterpart. This chapter, thus tries to look at Afghan women beyond Kabul or other urban pockets of the country and attempts to understand their predicament in comparison to their urban counterparts.

Third chapter, tries to deal with the relationship between the Afghan state, the society and the gender issues upto 2001. Emphasis was given to evaluate the socio-economic impact of three decades of war on Afghan women, particularly in reference to three period namely, the Communist rule, the Mujahideen period and the Taliban regime.

The *Fourth chapter*, explores the condition of women since the fall of Taliban regime. Year 2001, provided them with an opportunity to rewrite their history in a different way. The international intervention in Afghanistan by United States was justified on the basis of the requirement of addressing the gender related issues in the country. Subsequently, momentous decisions, amendments and laws were passed in favour of women, hoping that those will bring an end to the dark phases that proceeded before. This chapter attempts to look at some of those reforms and resolutions which were adopted to bring change in the lives of women and tries to understand how far those have been affective and how far the targets set have been realistic in the context of Afghansitan.

The Fifth chapter looks into the contemporary voices of women in Afghanistan. Several important organizations-Governmental, Non-Governmental, Civil Society organizations have been working on issues related to women. They have played significant roles in the advancements that have taken place in the past few years. Women are energetically engaged in every sector: at family counselling centers, as lawyers, social workers, as doctors, nurses teachers, health workers etc. This chapter highlights some of the success stories that can inspire people to think differently about contemporary Afghan women.

Chapter-I

A HISTORICAL OVERVIEW OF POSITION OF WOMEN IN AFGHANISTAN

> *"As for those who lead a righteous life, male or female, while believing, they*
> *enter Paradise; without the slightest injustice."*
>
> —*Al Qur'an* [4:124][65]

> "Religion does not require women to veil their hands, feet and faces or enjoin
> any special type of veil. Tribal custom must not impose itself on the free will of
> the individual."
>
> —Amanullah Khan, King of Afghanistan (1919–29)[66]

Over the past decades, Afghan women have been the subject to unprecedented levels of interest and international attention. There is a need to recognise the diversity of capacities and aspirations that exists within a group that comprises half a nation. Nancy Dupree describes this diversity in the following way:

> "It is useful perhaps to view the totality of Afghan women as a pyramid. The sound base is broad and consists of a majority who live in rural areas cherishing aspirations that are almost exclusively oriented towards children and family. Their needs lie in all aspects of basic and non-formal education, in health and in skill training for better family welfare. Here some

progress, albeit slow, is taking place in a non-confrontational manner.

At the tip are the small members of Western-oriented, assertive working women who have taken a leading part in the emancipation process begun in 1959. They have become accustomed to formal employment in mixed environments, often in association with foreigners who are now joined in battle on their behalf. These women call for the right to participate fully at all levels of decision-making. They bear the full brunt of Taliban ire.

In the centre is the solid core of professional teachers, medical practitioners, engineers, judges, administrators, businesswomen, social worker and civil servants of every sort which has grown in magnitude and strength since the beginning of the century. Largely from middle class, conservative but progressive families, these women neither wish to deny their society's values nor compromise Islam. Over the years they have shown by their comportment that Afghan women can function in the public sphere with no loss of dignity to themselves, their families or nation. Tragically, many have been lost to Afghanistan through resettlement. Many thousands remain, nevertheless, and thousands of others are being trained even though opportunities for utilizing their training look bleak. It is this strong central core that most urgently needs to be uncaged if Afghanistan is to recover and move forward."[67]

Afghan society traditionally has been characterised by conservative cultural norms in respect to women. This particular tradition of segregation, known as "purdah" among

Afghans can be described as an effort to maintain separation between men and women in public, and regulate the association between two sexes to different locations. This norm has traditionally assigned domestic roles in private spheres to women and public spheres to men. The practice of female seclusion has varied with circumstances like age, education, class, wealth and ethnicity. Geography has also played its share of role as there has been considerable variation in practice between urban and rural areas. Indigenous concepts of 'honour' and 'shame' traditionally have been reinforced in times of war and exile, with the honour and standing of men being determined, in the eyes of their peers, by the protection and modesty of "their" women.[68]

Afghan leaders have addressed themselves to the subject of reform for women for over a hundred years. These spokespersons, predominantly male, have held that nationalist ideology encompassing emancipation for women is essential to the creation of a progressive image for the nation.

Modern Monarchies

The birth if modern Afghanistan is attributed to Abdur Rahman Khan who ruled from 1880 to 1901. He was a descendant from a line of Pashtuns who largely controlled Afghanistan. Amir Abdur Rehman was the first ruler to attempt consolidation of the nation into a centralised state. He ruled with a ruthless hand that led to him being termed as the "Iran Amir". Yet, he attempted to alter some of the customary laws that were detrimental to women's status. He introduced many laws in an attempt to align customary social practices with the prescription of Islam.[69] He forbade child marriages, forced marriages, exorbitant bride prices and marriage gifts. He restored hereditary rights to widows and permitted women to seek divorce. He granted freedom in case of non-support and authorised the "mehr" (marriage gift) according to dictates of Quran. Even though he considered women subservient to men, he still felt that they were "due just treatment".[70] Nancy Hatch Dupree surmises that his liberal wife Bobo Jan may have influenced the Amir, pointing out that, "In fact, she was the first Afghan queen to appear in public in European dress without a veil. She rode horses and trained her maidservants in military exercises. She had keen interest in politics and went on numerous delicate missions to discuss politics between contending parties."[71] However, it was Abdur Rahman Khan who imposed the death penalty for adulterous women (which was contrary to the Quran) and decreed that men were entitled to full control over their women because "... the honour of the people of Afghanistan consists in the honour of their women."[72]

Upon the death of Amir, his son Amir Habibullah Khan took over and reigned for ten years. Habibullah continued his father's progressive agenda by putting a ceiling on extravagant marriage expenses that often caused poverty in many families. His wives wore western clothes and were seen without veils in public. In 1903, Habibullah established the first collage in Afghanistan, Habibiya Collage, employing foreign teachers from India, Turkey and Germany. [73] His other achievements included setting up of the first hospital, the first hydro electric plant, factories and construction of reads in Afghanistan and improved trade with Central Asia and India.[74]

The concept that women should be considered as contributing members of society beyond motherhood was first introduced during the reign of Amir Habibullah (1901-1919). Another significant contribution of Habibullah was the return of Afghan exiles including Majmud Beg Tarzi around the turn of the century. Mahmud Beg Tarzi, who was one of Afghanistan's greatest intellectuals and is regarded as the 'Father of Afghan Journalism' argued against overly protective restrictions on women and for education, pleading that egalitarian Islam does not deny women education and that is an Islamic duty to provide them with the opportunity to function fully in society. Only with educated women in the home, he said, could the family remain strong and the nation progress. To bolster his arguments, he published accounts of famous women through history in his news paper *Seraj-ul-Akhbar i Afghan (*The lamp of the news of Afghanistan).[75] Tarzi returned from Syria and became the editor of a modernist-nationalist newspaper which advocated political views critical to Western imperialism and in a subtle way the monarchy.[76]

Educated in Syria and Turkey, Tarzi was strongly influenced by modern interpretations of Islamic jurisprudence and by the liberties afforded to women in these countries. Convinced of women's abilities to engage in public professions, Tarzi viewed women as people who deserved full citizenship; he claimed that educated women were an asset to future generations and concluded that Islam did not deny equal rights. He devoted a special section on women's issues in his newspaper entitled "Celebrating Women of the world", which was edited by his wife Asma Tarzi. As Schinasi concludes, "no one before Tarzi had pronounced such words as 'liberty', 'respect for the homeland and religion', 'union', 'progress' or ' school' in Afghanistan."[77]

Habibullah, because of Tarzi'a liberal influence, opened a school for girls with English curriculum which tribal leaders and mullahs saw as going against the grain of tradition. Unfortunately as reflected by Magnus and Naby, "the liberalization of nation through education and modernization of even the 'tiny elite' spawned an opposition movement."[78] The religious leaders read Tarzi's articles and essays with increasing displeasure and contented that education for women would lead to the breakdown of the family, sexual anarchy and the ultimate degradation of women. They feared that this trend would lead to loss of honour of the nation. Education for women and state's interference in marriage institutions challenged the power of tribal leaders and their patrilineal and patrilocal kinship systems, resulting is Habibullahs's assassination in 1919.[79] Schinasi sums up Habibullah's reign perfectly, "Habibullah is sometimes referred to as the forgotten king, but it was Habibullah who was keen to maintain Afghanistan's position on the international as well as on the Muslim scene, but he was unable to control both with the same skill."[80]

The First Era of Change

After the assassination of Habibullah, his son Amanullah was placed on throne and his reign proved to be a turning point which saw full fledged modernization period of Afghanistan. His foremost attempt was to completely liberate Afghanistan from the British control and succeeded by defeating the British in the third and final Anglo-Afghan war in 1919. He relentlessly wanted to escort Afghanistan to the path of modernization and his agenda included liberation of Afghan women from tribal cultural norms. His exuberance and perseverance in enforcing these changes were heavily influenced by the modernization agenda operating in Turkey and his impressions from his travels in Europe.

Conservative aversion erupted into open revolt as King Amanullah attempted to institutionalize reform for women during his decade long tenure at the throne. Despite Amir Abdur Rahman's efforts, unjust and customary laws and practices continued to function in Afghanistan. He, therefore once again pressed to abolish child marriages, forced marriages, the leverite and to assure widow's rights.[81]Exorbitant marriage gifts were ordered curtailed. In addition, Amanullah attempted to go further by advocating monogamy, the removal of the veil, the end of seclusion and compulsory education for girls.[82]

In 1923, Amanullah drew up the first constitution, establishing the basis for the formal structure of the government and setting up the role of the monarch within the constitutional framework.[83] He was also influenced by Tarzi's sophisticated intellectual ideology in his endeavours. Tarzi was specifically instrumental in designing and implementing changes pertaining to women through his personal example of monogamy, education and employment of family members and their unveiled public appearances. [84] Later King Amanullah even married Mahmud Tarzi'a daughter Soraya.

Queen Soraya and his sister, Seraj-ul-Banat, were the first Afghan women to speak out publically on the subject. They had learnt their lessons well from the liberal-minded men around them. Speaking in 1923, Seraj ul-Banat said :

> "Some people are laughing at us, saying that women know only how to eat and drink. Old women discourage young women by saying their mothers never starved to death because they could not read or write... But knowledge is not man's monopoly. Women also deserve to be knowledgeable. We must on the one hand bring up healthy children and on the other hand, help men in their work. We must read about famous women in this world, to know that women can achieve exactly what men can achieve."[85]

Queen Soraya, spoke to women during the 1926 *Jeshyn* (Independence Day Celebration) even more forthrightly:

> "Independence has been achieved. It belongs to all of us...Do not think, however, that our nation needs only men to serve it? Women should also take part as women did in early years of our nation and Islam. The valuable services rendered by women are recounted throughout history from which we learn that women were not created solely for pleasure and comfort. From their examples we learn that we must all contribute towards the development of our nation and that this cannot be done without being equipped with knowledge. So, we should all attempt to acquire as much knowledge as possible in order that we may render our services to society in the manner of women of early Islam."[86]

Amanullah publicly campaigned against veil, against polygamy and encouraged education of girls not just in Kabul but also in country side. Amanullah even said that Islam did not require women to cover their bodies or wear any special kind of veil at a public function and by the time he finished his speech, Queen Soraya tore off her veil in public and apparently wives of other important officials who were present there also did the same. Many women from Amanullah's family publicly participated in different organizations and went on to become government officials later in their lives. Amanullah's sister, Kobra, who formed the *Anjuman-i-Himayat-i-Niswan*, (organization for women's protection) in 1920s. This organization worked towards injustices against women and encouraged them to bring their complaints to the organization and to unite to contest the oppressive institutions. Another sister founded a hospital for women. Queen Soraya along with her mother initiated the first magazine for women called *Ershad-i-Nishan* (Guidance for Women). Education of women was taken very seriously and to give impetus to this endeavour fifteen young women were sent to Turkey to acquire Higher Education in 1928. Soraya's contribution can hardly be exaggerated as far as enforcing changes in the lives of Afghan women are concerned. She encouraged and inspired women of her times to actively participate in the nation building process.

During the later part of Amanullah's reign, the King and Queen visited Europe where they were honoured and felicitated. During his 'Grand Tour' in 1927, he and the Queen visited India, Egypt, Italy, France, Germany, Britain, Soviet Union and Iran. Martin Ewans write that in all these countries, they made a considerable impression, if only because Afghanistan was a relatively unknown country and it came as a pleasant surprise to find it is ruled by an engaging amiable and outgoing king, accompanied by an attractive consort.[87] In 1928 Oxford University even awarded them honorary degrees.[88] They were particularly impressed by Europe and changes in Turkey. After returning to Afghanistan they attempted to implement some of the social and cultural changes they had experienced in the western society to their own society back home. He was determined to transform Afghanistan into a 'Modern' society. This was also a time when some other Muslim countries like Turkey and Egypt were also going through the process of transformation and were on the path of modernization. The elite section of the Afghan society was particularly impressed to witness these changes in other countries, attempted to emulate their development models. However Afghanistan was not ready for such changes. While the King and the Queen were away from the country a British source distributed pictures of the Queen without veil, dining with foreign men, and having her hand kissed by the leader of France among tribal regions of Afghanistan. Conservative mullahs and regional leaders took the images and details from the royal family's trip to be a flagrant betrayal of Afghan culture, religion and 'honour' of women.[89] Some of the historians have even viewed the circulation of picture from foreign source as an evidence of British effort to destabilize the Afghan monarchy as first of many international attempts to keep the country in political, social and economic turmoil. Eventually when the royal family returned, they encountered hostility and were eventually forced out of office.

In August 1928 Amanullah convened a *Loya Jirga* (Grand Assembly of Tribal Leaders) in Kabul and presented his policies on social, cultural, political and economic reforms including rights and equality of women and fighting administrative corruption as bureaucrats used their positions to collect bribes and kickbacks.[90] In that meeting Queen Soraya accompanied him to the hall of the *Jirga* without her veil. An estimated one hundred women, who were accompanying the Queen also discarded their veil to the praise and applause of progressive delegates.[91] As expected, just the opposite response was seen from the conservatives and traditionalists who were scandalised by this action, calling it a transgression against Islamic values. At the *Jirga*, though representatives reluctantly endorsed Amanullahs's proposals but finally put their foot down when marriage age of girls were raised to 18 years and for men to 21 years. Because of strong opposition Amanullah had to reverse some of his policies and conform to more traditional social change but it was too late by then as mobilizing of public opinion against the king and his state policies had started by that time.

Some of Amanullah's modernization endeavours had no practical application to the daily lives of common people. Inhabitants of Kabul were ordered to wear western attire, which often were very expensive and turned out to be huge burden for poor people living in the city. To ensure its implementation, harsh measures were adopted- signs were posted in the areas of the city that prohibited entry to veiled women, and law enforcement officers fined anyone who did not obey the orders.[92] The first women's theatre was established in Paghman, Kabul, in 1921 in an effort to provide women with a respite from their normal and often boring routine of looking after children and performing household chores.[93]

Amanullah tried to consolidate Islam and state policies but faltered when he tried to impose rapid changes pertaining to women's status. His conservative countrymen in rural areas felt the reforms were too "western" for society and the forced changes were against the doctrine of Islam. Resistance came from several quarters but the strangest opposition came to the abolition of bride price and polygamy and to the introduction of girls education. 1920s therefore saw a struggle between elite modernists and traditional tribals and the main bone of contention was the changing status of women. What came as a huge shock was the law in 1924 by which women could choose their own partners and attempts were made to abolish bride price. Fathers of young women saw such progressive laws as a loss of social status, familial control and financial security.[94]

These modernization programmes, after some time were being interpreted as 'un-Islamic' and counter to traditional values. While overt focus went to superimposing modernization from above, crucial aspects such as army, economic degradation, growing corruption were ignored. The first reality check came in the form of the rebellion in Khost in 1925, however state succeeded in suppressing it.[95] But opposition continued to mount stating that he and his wife were attempting to undermine Islamic values by promoting western culture and called for a *Jihad* to restore Islamic order.

Schools of girls in Kabul were closed down and women had to revert to wearing veils. As Valentine Moghadam points out, women could not cut their hair, mullahs were given unlimited powers to instate their agendas and the old tribal system was to be reinstated.[96] Amanullah even married for the second time (for a brief period) to pacify the opposition, but it was too late. In 1929 conservative religious and tribal leaders spearheaded the revolution which overthrew King Amanullah. Georgian asserts that, "Amanullah, determined to improve this situation (the status of women) and maintaining that his support of the feminist cause was based on the true tenets of Islam, took more steps in the direction in his short rule than were taken by his predecessors together."[97] Amanullah was undoubtedly ahead of his time liberalism in an era when Afghanistan was barely united in the sense of nationhood was traumatic for the state.[98]

The next two decades saw the Afghan royalty change hands with different families and leaders, but not again a leader who would push the reform and women's agenda to the detriment of their rule. To restore the sanctity of Islam and the honour of the nations, Amanullah's successor, Habibullah Ghazi (Bacha Saqqao, January to October 1929) to Nadir Shah (1929 to 1933), who ousted him, insisted upon a return to reactionary customs regarding women. In 1930s and 1940s, Afghan women saw a cautious introduction of rights. In 1931 Nadir Shah announced the second Constitution and opened schools for girls and tried to bring about some gender based reforms but at the same time was careful to avoid conflicts with mullahs and tribal leaders. Despite his cautious steps on gender issues, Nadir Shah was assassinated and his son Zahir Shah came to power. Seclusion of women continued until 1959 as they continued to wear *Chadri* (veil). Howver the concept that women should participate in national development was reintroduced as a national policy. Separate schools were established and education for women gradually gained respectability. Women were employed in professions considered appropriate for them, as teachers, medical personnel and administrators in female institutions.[99]

Post Monarchy Period

By mid-century, with massive foreign aid and technical assistance from the Soviet Union, Afghanistan embarked on the modernizing journey. By the late 1950s, a need was perceived for women to be economically active to help Afghanistan achieve its targeted development goals. Women's issues were once again getting attention and were given some consideration. When, therefore, the government of Prime Minister Daoud (1953-1963) launched a revolution for women in 1959 by announcing its support of the voluntary removal of the veil and an end to seclusion, Afghan women were well-prepared to take their place in multifaceted activities.[100] Conservative elements in the society who protested were jailed and challenged to provide Quranic proof, not interpretations for their objection.[101] Since that was not forthcoming the evolutionary process towards emancipation began.

Prime Minister Daud did not want to repeat the haste and mistakes of his predecessor Amanullah and accordingly declared veiling a "voluntary option". Women in this period of time in Afghanistan were again expected to abandon the veil, marriage expenses were also curtailed and were expected to contribute to the economy. Afghan women also felt encouraged to take part in the various activities in the changed political environment. They were automatically enfranchised, without a suffragette movement, by the 1964 Constitution (third) which stated that all Afghans "without discrimination of preference, have equal rights and obligations before the law."[102] Among other things the new constitution guaranteed women "dignity, compulsory education and freedom to work".[103] With this development women started entering politics as well. The first woman Minister was in the health department, elected to the Parliament along with three other women.[104] Progress continued without further strident demonstrations, but at the same time age old customary beliefs and customs prevailed, even among the enlightened. The government of Republic of Afghanistan, founded by Mohamad Daud in 1973, attempted to redress specific problems through a Penal Code (1976) and Civil Law (1977), both of which followed the constitutional injunction that: "There can be no law repugnant to the basic principles of the sacred religion of Islam...".[105]

In 1965 People's Democratic Party of Afghanistan (PDPA), a Soviet backed socialist organization was formed. The same year also saw the formation of first women's group- the Democratic Organization of Afghan Women (DOAW). Foremost objective of this group was to spread education among women, ban forced marriages and do away with bride the price. Over the years increasing number of educated women emerged to work in government and private sectors, as secretaries and judges, hair dressers and diplomats, entertainers and parliamentarians.[106] They were also seen in factories, including ceramics. Fruit packaging, pharmaceuticals and housing construction, however this is not to suggest that they were engaged in manual labour. Girl students also went abroad for studying. The direction therefore was positive and steady, but because of Government's insistence on voluntary acceptance of change, the numbers was not too extensive and those who joined hailed from middle of upper strata of urban communities. Even within the overall sense on progress undercurrents of dissent existed.

The Second Era of Change

The second era of intense women's reform occurred in the late 1970s. The year 1978 saw the rise to power of the controversial PDPA.[107] It was during the PDPA rule that rapid social and economic change, echoing some of the 1920s theme, was implemented and mass literacy campaign not only for women but men of all age was introduced.[108] Massive land reform programmes, and abolition of bride price and raising marriage were part of PDPA agenda. In October 1978 a decree was issued with the explicit intension of ensuring equal rights for women. Age limit of 16 for girls and 18 for boys were set. Yet another time, the revolutionary pace of social change started creating problems for conservative mullahs and tribal chiefs of the interiors. In 1968, the conservative members of parliament proposed to enact a law that would prohibit girls from going abroad for education. To this move, hundreds of demonstrating girls vociferously brought their constitutional guarantee of equal rights to the attention of the parliamentarians.[109] In 1970, two conservative mullahs protested specific traits of women's liberation like wearing of mini-skirts, women teachers etc by shooting at the legs of women dressed in Western dress and splashing them with acid.[110] In April, 5000 girls fearful that the legal system, dominated by males who were often conservatives, took to streets in Kabul. The first demonstrations by women were early indicators that women's consciousness was developing. Batya Swift Yasgur in her book *Behind the Burqa,* translated the stories of two sisters Sulima and Hala and their lives in Afghanistan. Sulima, a teenager from Kabul during the 1970s depicted the enthusiasm among women of her age towards women's organization and the cause of literacy among women. She like many others used to campaign for girls education against the wish of her father.

Sulima shares, "I spoke to girls at school about how education could give them a better life. I told them stories about places where women could read and write, could hold jobs, could be free...if families could not afford to do so, we raised money and also helped them out with supplies such as notebooks, pens and books...I am proud to have been associated with this first women's movement in Afghanistan."[111] As Marsden points out, "The PDPA's use of force in bringing the changes to fruition, combined with a brutal disregard for societal and religious sensitivities, resulted in massive backlash from the rural population."[112]

Though the law enforced during that period included familiar articles against practices like child marriages, forced marriages, abandonment protected inheritance and declared 'mehr' to be the property of wife, yet a number of sex-discriminating social customs that encouraged male domination in matters of divorce, adultery and defence of honour were preserved by their entrenchment in these legal statuses. As Nancy Dupree points out, many attitudes reflected in the laws, both positive and negative, had been subject to argument between Muslim traditionalist and modernists for centuries.[113] Situation was particularly critical for families which allowed partial emancipation while insisting on patriarchal control as an ideal. Expected complexities were visible, when on one hand girls were allowed to get educated and then denied the right to express her opinion of for that matter exercise her choice to work outside home. This partial liberalization was creating basis for disgruntlement which naturally fostered incipient rebellion.

Dupree has pointed out that this insistence on patriarchal control arose in part from the fact that in Afghanistan women symbolize honour, of the nation and family. Any deviation from honourable behaviour on the part of the women as it is defined by any given family or group is seen to besmirch the honour of those in authority and cannot, therefore, be tolerated.[114] It is this attitude, according to Dupree that has perpetuated overly protective institutions and customs, such as the veil and seclusion.

Women in Afghanistan by that time had begun to ask questions on precise definition, in modern terms, of exactly what constituted 'honourable behaviour' on their part. They were conscious of the fact they had been asked to contribute to national development and enhance image of progressive Afghanistan. They had accepted this ideology presented to them by men and responded with distinction, functioning with poise and dignity, with no loss of honour to themselves of to their families, and with much credit to the nation.[115] But with education comes empowerment and Afghan women became increasingly aware of the importance of their roles and started examining opportunities as individuals rather that stereotypes or national symbols. They were ready to be released from the practice of family consensus and given the right to take crucial decisions as individuals and thereby began to articulate goals in conflict with male-oriented ideas. The government, though provided required safeguards and assistance to them and their causes, was still at that point unable and unwilling to insist on breaking restrictions imposed by the family that remained the single most important institution in Afghan society. Reforms were implemented only up to a point.

While this was a truth, the fact that women s issues captured the centre stage during the turbulent democratic , Soviet backed regime cannot be denied. With reasonable backing from the government, during this era women started getting employment, in significant numbers, at Universities, private corporations, the airlines and also as doctors and nurses. However the nation as a whole was experiencing destruction and anarchy. An Afghan protégé of USSR, Hafizullah Amin, dismissed as many conservatives as he could find and formed a Revolutionary Council in Kabul to initiate Marxist programme of scientific socialism . This was a prelude to the full-scale conflict of December 1979, as 50,000 Red Army soldiers from USSR marched into Afghanistan. Moscow immediately installed in Afghanistan their favourite Babrak Karmal as President. In response the US entered into the scene and poured in a large amount of aid in order to assist the Afghans opposed to the communist rule in their country. The aid was channelled through Pakistan to thousands of Mujahideen (holy warriors) who were undergoing training to fight the Soviet. With these developments, external forces like Iran, Saudi Arabia, China also found enough motivation to entered into the picture. The Afghan countryside was the breeding ground for these freedom fighters . Suspicious of the Soviet socialist agenda to annihilate the traditional culture and religion of Afghanistan, the Mujahideen was able to gather forces to form their own revolutionary army.[116] 'War in the name of Islam' was their battle cry also emphasised a reversal of all socialist policies including those that guaranteed women liberties through education and empowerment.

After the Soviet withdrawal in 1989 and the eventual dissolution of the Soviet Union in 1991, several efforts were made to agree on an effective governmental mechanism but time and again these efforts failed. Civil war broke out between various rival factions and no mechanismss on power-sharing agreement could be instituted. In 1992 however, the Mujahideen took over Kabul and declared Afghanistan an Islamic state. According to US Department of State (1995), "In

1992 women were increasingly precluded from public service. In conservative areas in 1994, many women appeared in public only if dressed in a complete head-to-toe garment with a mesh covered opening for their eyes."[117] As Hala, a young girl in Afghanistan during that period recalled in the book *Behind the Burqa* how at this point of time her family encouraged her to devote more time to the practice of Islam. "Turning to religion provided some inner peace but did very little to lessen my fear of the Mujahideen",[118] she also added "...the fact that I was now a practicing Muslim did not give me anything in common with the Mujahideen just because they were also Muslims- their version of religion and mine were completely different...theirs was about fear and coercion, about punishment and haltered being practiced in the name of Islam."The author of *Zoya's Story* claimed. "Far from rejoicing that the Russians had been defeated, Grandmother told me that a worse Devil had come to my country. There was a popular saying around this time: "Rid us of these seven donkeys and give us back our cow. They donkeys were the seven factions of the Mujahideen and the cow was the puppet regime of (Najibullah who was installed by the Russians before they left.)"[119] According to Zoya, The Mujanhideen entered Kabul and burnt down the University, library and schools and forced women to wear burqa and consequently fewer women were visible in public space. The period from 1992-1996 saw unprecedented barbarism by the Mujahideen, where stories of killing, rapes, amputations and other forms of violence became common.

Eventually, the Taliban, a group of radical Islamic students emerged in the Afghan political scene in 1994 and within a stint of two years, established control over ninety percent of Afghan territory. Initially a sense of relief was palpable. But it was extremely short lived and without wasting much time they set up *Amar Bil Maroof Wa Nahi An Al-Munkar* (Department for the Promotion of Virtue and Prevention of Vice) to monitor and control women's behaviour.[120] It brought sweeping changes in the social order and used radio to propagate its new laws. Radio Sharia was used by the fundamentalist regime to remind the men and women of Afghanistan, their duties towards Islam and listed the changes they need to make in their lifestyle. For women, this meant no longer being able to go outside except to buy food and if at all they had to leave they had to be accompanied by a *mahram* or close male relative. They were forbidden from most of the privileges they had enjoyed few years back. Much criticised by the international community, for such radical policies, dogmatic adherence and imposition of Sharia, particularly the policies of gender discrimination, the Taliban did not enjoy recognition by the international community except by three countries, viz. Pakistan, UAE and Saudi Arabia. However Nancy Hatch Dupree observed that Afghan women continued to be involved in the political arena even when Taliban were around. In 1996, she writes, 150 poor beggar women demonstrated in front of the governor's office in Kandahar, and successfully persuaded the governor to order shopkeepers to accept small bank notes, or they would be closed. Later in 1996 in Kabul, when Taliban protested against foreign interference, a female judge in General Dostam's administration provided inspiration as women held a five hour rally in Mazar-e-Sharif producing slogans such as "Taliban law is not Islamic Law". Towards the end of 1996 in Herat, 50 women protested the closing of women's bath houses. Several were beaten and 20 were arrested.[121] However even these were completely stopped once they issued decrees on a range of matters for both men and women once they gained control over 90 percent of the land. The period that was witnessed from 1996 to 2001, was one of its kind especially in terms of the policies they adopted for women. Though throughout the civil war period women in Afghanistan witnessed terrible times and a 'change' from that order was not completely uncalled for but what replaced the dreaded civil war period was something unprecedented.

The Taliban Period – Neoprivatization of women?

The society created by the Taliban in Afghanistan between 1996 and 2001 constantly evoked outrage and disbelief from Western press. Even the Ayatollahs in Tehran issued a statement condemning the Taliban for defaming Islam by confusing it with medieval obscurantism.[122] Peter Marsden said that "there are no easy labels with which to define the Taliban. Since the Taliban are mostly Pushtun and rural, they are, in part, influenced by the code of honor in Pashtun Law. Thus they are concerned that girls will be corrupted if they are taught anything other than pure Islam. They seeked to return society to the way it was before Daoud's reforms, the PDPA Coup and fourteen years of the Soviets and rule by Islamist parties and preserve the Western agencies."[123] The word "Taliban" literally mean "student" in Arabic. However, in Persian this plural form of "*talib*" means "religious student". The word is merely applied to those who seek religious scholarship in traditional circles of learning, namely *madrrasahs*.[124] The Taliban had set out as an Islamic reform movement. Throughout Muslim history, Islamic reform movements have transformed both the nature of belief and political and social life, as Muslim nomadic tribes destroyed other Muslim empires, transformed them, and then were themselves urbanized and later destroyed. This political change has always been made possible through the concept of Jihad.[125] The overwhelming Pashtun (ethnic majority in Afghanistan)

Taliban took and kept power by military means, instituting rule by militia, but their authority was enhanced by religious charisma as holy men.[126] They fought with other ethnic groups such as Shiite Hazaras, the Tajiks and Uzbeks (who formed the opposition Northern Alliance), demonstrated their power, as did events like the massacres of defeated populations in the town of Mazar-e-Sharif and Bamyan. They revived the public executions as spectacle as part of their implementation of power as public performance. Even the tapes from music and vedeocassettes were torn from their casing and displayed on the goalposts of the stadium where executions were held.[127]Journalist Jan Goodwin witnessed a Taliban spectacle early in 1998:

> "Thirty-thousand men and boys poured into the dilapidated Olympic sports stadium in Kabul. Street hawker peddled nuts, biscuits and tea to the waiting crowd. The scheduled entertainment? They were there to see a young woman, Sohaila, receive 100 lashes and to watch two thieves have their right hand amputed. Sohaila had been arrested walking with a man who was not a relative, a sufficient crime for her to be guilty of adultery. Since she was single, it was punished by flogging; had she been married, she would have been publicly stoned to death... As Sohaila. Completely covered in the shroud-like *burqa* veil, was forced to kneel and then flogged, Taliban "cheerleaders" had the stadium ringing with the chants of onlookers. Among those present there were just three women: the young Afghan, and two female relatives who had accompanied her. The crowd fell silent only when the luckless thieves were driven into the arena and pushed to the ground...Holding the severed hands aloft by the index fingers, a grinning Taliban fighter warned the huge crowd, *These are the chopped-off hands of thieves, the punishment for any of*

> *you caught stealing*. Then to restore the party atmosphere the thieves were driven in jeep once around the stadium, a flourish that brought the crowd to their feet, as was intended. These Friday circuses, at which Rome's Caligula would doubtless have felt at home, are to become weekly fixtures for the entertainment-starved male residents of Kabul."[128]

According to Peter Marsden, there were four main elements to the Taliban policy: a ban on the employment of women, except in health sector; a temporary halt to formal female education pending the drawing up of an appropriate curriculum; the imposition of strict codes on both women and men requiring women to wear burqas and men to wear beard, unstyled hair, turbans and *shalwar kameez*; and the introduction of strict controls on the movement of women outside the homes so that they are always separated from male strangers or are escorted by male relatives.[129] However the Taliban had stated that they will consider allowing women to work once they have made arrangements allowing women and men to work separately and travel separately.[130] Mullah Omar and the Taliban claimed legitimacy as the guarantors of Sharia, and said that it was their duty to conform the bodies of Afghans to its structures. A young women memoirist, Zoya, reports, "Near the stadium, we saw their patrols ordering shopkeepers to close down and go watch the ritual. I was surprised to see women taking their children with them, but (my friend) Zeba explained, 'They want their children to realize what will happen to them if they ever steal anything.' They think scaring people is a good way to educate them."[131]

There were several instances of public thrashing, delivered to a group of women in the street, upheld the caste like privileges of Taliban and the sanctity of their flag and one such instance was depicted by a woman named Latifa. She saw a group of women in long black veils being beaten bloody by Taliban in the street. Bewildered, she later made inquiries. "they were beaten because they were wearing white socks...that is the colour of Taliban flag, and women do not have the right to wear white. It means they are defiling the flag."[132]Juan R. I. Cole has argued that the highly publicized destruction by the Taliban (apparently at the insistence of bin Laden and al-Qaeda) of the Buddhas of Bamiyan in the spring of 2001 was not merely a statement of religious iconoclasm, given the idols are forbidden in the Taliban version of Islam, in a way it was also functioned as a further assertion of power of spectacle.[133] In a way Taliban used to enjoy defying the outrage of international community. The Taliban were not the first Muslim iconoclasts to wreak damage on pre-Islamic art and monuments in Afghanistan, but they were the first to do it in so spectacular and systematic a manner.[134]

The restriction that both Afghan men and women experienced during the Taliban regime extreme. Men were given six weeks to grow beard to a hands length and to trim their moustaches in accordance with a literal reading of sayings about the Prophet Muhammad's appearance. While many accepted the new rule comfortably, for many it was the compulsion that forced them to adopt these. A young female memoirist Latifa, of her life during the Taliban reported that her middle class father complied with the new rule, grumbling, "My beard belongs to the Taliban, not to me!"[135] In Taliban terminology, what was *Zaher*, or public, had to conform to their understanding of Sharia as interpreted by medieval jurists. The beard was public, could be seen and so required conformity. Latifa also mentioned about how the state interfered on a man's most personal decision of having a haircut in a particular style. She shares an interesting story to indicate how men's bodies became an arena of contention between globalization consumer culture and the Taliban localization. It was around this time the Hollywood film *Titanic* was making waves across the world, such was the popularity of the movie that even Taliban Afghanistan was impacted, as many young Afghan boys wanted to look like the protagonist of the film. Latifa wrote that "the Titanic fashion wrought ravages, notably among the barbers and as a response Radio Sharia announced that 28 of them were arrested and condemned for having given young men a Di Caprio haircut."[136]

The Egyptian journalist Fahmi Huwaydi reported about the text of decree by the Ministry for the Promotion of Virtue and the Prevention of Vice issued in December 17, 1996, at the order of Mullah Omar, banning sixteen activities:

1. Temptation *(fitna)* likely to cause public disturbance and the baring of women's faces in public was forbidden. Taxi drivers were not to accept as fares women who wore a burqa but did not completely cover their faces, on pain of imprisonment. Women were not to walk in the street without a close male relative *(mahram)*.
2. Music was forbidden in the shops, hotels, and automobiles, on pain of imprisonment and the closing of the offending establishment.
3. Shaving a beard was forbidden. A month and a half after the decree, anyone not bearded was to be imprisoned until his beard grew out.
4. Daily prayers were to be said in mosques. Shops had to be closed at prayer time and the vehicles had to cease circulating in the streets 15 minutes before prayer time. Shopkeepers pen at prayer time would be jailed for 10 days.
5. Training pigeons and playing with birds were forbidden.
6. Drug trafficking was forbidden, along with the use of drugs.
7. Kite flying and betting on it was forbidden.

8. No image of persons could be displayed in shops, hotels or taxis, since this was a form of idolatry.
9. Gambling was forbidden.
10. Letting one's hair grow out in the American or British fashion was forbidden. The agents of the Ministry for Promotion of Virtue and Prevention of Vice were to apprehend violators and cut their hair.
11. Taking interest on loan was forbidden, on pain of a long prison term.
12. Women were not to wash clothes on the banks of rivers. If found doing so they would be remanded to the custody of male guardian and severely punished.
13. Music and dancing were forbidden at wedding ceremonies.
14. Drum music was forbidden. The ulama (boy of clerics) would decide on the punishment for it.
15. Men were forbidden to tailor women's clothing or to take their measurements. If found doing so they would face a prison term.
16. Practicing astrology was forbidden. Astrologers would be imprisoned until the repented. Their books would be burned.[137]

Thus baring of women's faces in public, the display of images of women (for example of Bollywood actresses), the male tailoring of women's clothes, public washing etc were all banned. In some cases the Taliban were simply reimplementing older statutes. Women washing clothes in the river was banned by the Kabul municipality in the 1950s, and tailors had for some time been under suspicion because of their mixing with and easy access to women. Juan R. I. Cole, in his article has viewed this as extreme 'privatization of women'.[138] They not only attempted to push (law abiding) domesticity relentlessly into the private realm, but also coded the female body as inherently private. The neoprivatization of women formed a key goal of Taliban policy, as is clear in the autobiographical accounts of women like Latifa, Zoya and Sulima. However this is definitely not to suggest that gender segregation in Afghanistan was a novel concept in any way. Previous regimes have done this and this was any thing but new in Pashtun societies. But because they imposed this norm in urban societies and because of the extreme measures they took for implementation of the norm, it perhaps seems more draconian to city dwellers than in the past. Without much doubt, Taliban policy towards women reversed that of the communist government of 1980s.

The Taliban announced a policy of closing girl's schools and of confining women to their homes. This was the first step they took once they captured Kabul. Within three months, the Taliban had closed sixty-three schools, affecting 103,000 girls and somewhat more boys.[139] Mawlawi Said Shahifkhayl, the Taliban undersecretary of education in1 998, explained the regime's policy towards women to Egyptian journalist Huwaydi, where he said:

> "the education of girls requires a jurisprudential ruling *(Fatwa)* that would fix its path and its limits. As for women working outside the house, the text concerning that is clear and the matter is incontrovertible. For when the Koran says 'stay in your houses' [140][33:33; the feminine imperative is used], the issue requires no further discussion and we have nothing to do but obey."

However at the interview, the undersecretary mentioned that the ban on women's education was not a fixed policy, rather a temporary measure. The insistence that women remain within the four walls of their homes, however, was not only rigid policy, he said but the divine law and so was beyond discussion. When Huwaydi quoted to him a saying of the Prophet Muhammad that seeking knowledge is duty of every Muslim, Mawlawi responded by saying that there were two points to that. One was the saying specified only "Muslims", using the male for of the word and did not mention any female Muslim (*muslimah*). Secondly he said that the girls knew nothing of their religion and "had no interest in their roles as wives, mothers and mistresses of the family" He added that the appearances of the girls, the nature of the teaching staff, and the condition of the buildings all required extensive review.[141]

In the week after the Taliban took Kabul, women doctors were confined to their houses and denied permission to go out. Zoya points out that women patients suffered as a result, since they could not be seen by male physicians, and she said that a religious rationale was given for women being a sort of martyr if they died from lack of treatment. The Taliban rules affected the working class women the most, especially single women, orphans and war widows, especially hard. Some of the elements within the Islamic world that were opposed to the Taliban for political or strategic reasons took the opportunity created by international reactions to Taliban gender policies to level public criticism on them. Pakistan's Jamaat-i-Islami Party, issued a statement in which they said that the Taliban decree of barring women from education and employment, ordering women to wear the veil and requiring the men to grow beards could give negative image of Islam.[142]

As is known today, the policies of the Taliban have created particular dilemmas for Western agencies and the international community, who had quite naturally responded from the Western perspective as well as from the point of UN Human Rights Convention. However it must be kept in mid that Afghanistan is one of the few places left in the world where Western media did not penetrate to a significant degree. The rigidity of the Taliban gender policies could also be seen as a desperate attempt to keep out that other world and to protect Afghan women from influences that could weaken the society from within.[143]

While the Taliban could achieve control over a vast territory in a remarkably short period of time the fact remains that there were areas where it could not penetrate. In those regions therefore the conflict continued between the Taliban and the Northern Alliance who wanted to hold to the small bit of territory. Northern Alliance was comprised of Mujahideens, who were responsible for devastating the country before the Taliban came to power. On the liberation of Kabul in November 2001 therefore, Zoya states, "No one was sorry to see Taliban defeated, but neither did they rejoice when Northern Alliance (comprising of former Mujahideens) took over. They too had blood in their hands."[144]

Thus the two so called progressive eras in the history of Afghanistan, 1920s and 1970s, while attempting to improve women's status were not unsuccessful but also led to violent, fundamentalist backlashes by the subsequent governments. If both the phases are observed carefully, a definite pattern can be visible. In both the periods, tribal leaders who objected to the redefining of women by the state and the stepping-down of their general authority initiated the disruption of the modernization process. The modernization attempts in general were imposed from above and the steps taken symbolised that those were mare imitation of practices of other cultures, which were remarkably distinct and unsuitable for the Afghan scenario. The patterns of resistance to change focused on conditions for women also suggested that any effort of modernization in Afghanistan would succeed with full recognition of the multiple conflicts, fissures and resistances to change. Both the eras also attempted to forcibly impose change and in neither situation the desire, aspirations and preferences were taken into account. The Taliban era on the other hand witnessed a complete reversal of the trends set by the progressive eras. It was not for the first time though that Afghanistan was experiencing such strict adherence of Sharia or other Laws but the strictness in which those were implemented was something unseen before. This shook the international community among which only three countries recognised the Taliban government. Initially they tried to remain aloof from the developments within Afghanistan based on the argument that what was happening there was their internal matters, however as their measures became stricter and the degree of violence as well as violation of human rights increased, the international community could not remain a silent spectator anymore. Not only Western societies, Islamic Republic of Iran, which had been called medieval by its political opponents, criticized and condemned the Taliban.

The phases of Afghanistan's history which we discussed in this chapter, in a way mark a tussle between the tradition and modernity. Though it is hard to segregate any particular phase which had a homogeneous impact across Afghanistan, that is both in rural and urban areas of the country. However it will not be incorrect to see the 1920s and 1970s as phases that championed 'modern' way on life and encouraged the people to adopt changes which were mostly in tune with the Western definition of 'Modernism'. In the first phase (1920s) particularly, the inspiration behind the encouragement and adoption of changes by the state authority came from observation of Western societies, which were starkly different from its own. The 1970s on the other hand saw a different modernization drive, based on the belief that changes must be brought in the existing order, since to the Soviets it was the more acceptable 'way of life', something that they can relate to. In both the phases it did not matter, if the people of the country, most of whom residing in rural and tribal milieu actually identified with the imposed 'way of life'. Perhaps it not just the Western media or the international community, that tried to understand the requirement and aspiration of Afghans through the prism of *Kabulis (*inhabitant of Kabul) or other urban centres. The state authority in Afghanistan had committed similar slips. Coming to the more recent Taliban phase, Juan R. I Cole has used the term *counter-modernity* rather than *anti-modernism* to describe it because they adopted some key motifs from high modernism and their power depended on modern tools (the state, radio, mass spectacle, tank corps and machine guns mounted on Toyotas).[145] They used these tools for the purpose very different from the goals of the industrialised democracies, however with regard to the private domain. Their policies were most stringent in the urban centres of Afghanistan as they believed that the modernisation attempts had impacted these urban lives much more that their counterpart in rural areas. Though the policies were imposed across the land where they could establish their control yet the responses coming from the women in the urban and rural parts of the country were not alike. Like most countries, there remains a huge gap between the experiences of women in the rural and urban spaces of Afghanistan, the next section, would particularly explore that.

Chapter-II

BARRIERS AND BRIDGES: WOMEN IN RURAL AND URBAN AFGHANISTAN

Nancy Dupree notes that during 1960s and 1970s conditions of women varied widely depending on their socio-economic position and on whether they lived in an urban or rural environment. The changes which were brought by the state authority during 1920s and 1970s, that is the two progressive eras discussed in the previous chapter essentially touched the lives of the women in the major cities. By the end of 1970s, amongst the middle and upper class elite, many Kabuli women were able to move freely around the city without a male family member. They regarded education as their right, studied at universities and expected to have their own career. However the reaction that was produced amongst the conservative religious leaders, feudal land lords and Mullahs (clerics) across the country, compelled the political dispensation in Kabul to temporarily resist some of the reforms and modify several others. Modifications came in the form of directing women to receive schooling at home, encouraging religious studies prior to learning foreign languages, allowing men to marry four wives etc. However these concessions and others did not appease the tribal chiefs and conservative clerics and they continued their opposition till the reforms were withdrawn. But even while these developments were happening the section of women population which were affected by these were primarily the women from affluent or middle class of urban Afghanistan.

Nevertherless, even in the 1970s, amongst the lower-middle and lower classes, who still comprised a majority of city's population, most women seldom left their homes without a male escort, even to go for shopping.[146] Within this segment of urban society there were rarely interactions between men and women other than on domestic issues, men would go out to work in factories or in offices, while the women would remain at home. In the old city particularly, houses were built around inward-looking courtyards, arranged in neighbourhoods that were divided ethnically, geographically and in kin-oriented sections, where social cohesiveness was strong and the lives of most women were tightly confided. These houses in the main cities like Kabul had to host their extended family members from rural areas, mostly the male members who had come to cities to acquire advanced education at Universities. The book *Behind the Burqa,* describes such dwellings and how unrelated guests were accommodated in smaller houses separated from the main building- the guest house, or *mehmankhana,* which generally overflowed with guests in compliance with Afghan tradition of *mehmannawazi.* The presence of all these guests meant endless housework for the women. Sulima, from a moderately progressive family in Kabul in the early 70s described, "We (female members of the family) did all the laundry for all members of the household, including residents of the *mehmankhana* At mealtime, we served the guests, then withdrew. I myself started doing housework when I was just about six years old... I was taught to wash cups and spent much time of the day at the sink. Needless to say, the endless procession of guests led to an endless stream of dishes, which the women were endlessly washing.[147]"

By contrast, life in the rural villages, where the majority of Afghanistan's women lived and remains very different. Nancy

Dupree in an interview given to the Swedish Committee for Afghanistan publication expressed how her experience of living in rural Afghanistan changes the prevalent view that Afghan women were repressed drastically. It did not take long for her to realise that "all these prejudices about Afghan women were 100 percent false." She learned to see the strength of the rural woman. She witnessed mutual respect between men and women. She heard women say to their husbands who wanted to have a meal put on table: "I'm busy with something else, make your own lunch."[148]

Afghanistan beyond Kabul[150]

Vast stretches of the Afghan landscape are dominated by mountainous terrain leaving many villages remote and extremely isolated, accessible only on foot, donkey or horseback. Such villages are commonly inhabited by one kin-oriented section of the community, with most inhabitants related to one another, either by blood or by marriages and consequently falling into the *mehram* category of male-female relationships.[151] As a result, poor rural Afghan women typically may enjoy considerably more freedom of movement than their counterparts in the urban areas since they are essentially parts of large extended families. Villages on the plains, which tend to be larger and more diverse, follow more urban patterns of settlements, with housing arranged in largely kin-oriented wards.[152] Women generally move freely between these family units and some older women, who emerge as trusted leaders, may be able to pass between different kinship sections. Afghanistan is a patriarchal society where kinship play a prominent role in mobilizing public support and developing alliances. Polygamy is a common practice among affluent rural and urban families, as it helps wealthy men expand their social networks and power by creating alliances.[153]

Primary Roles of Women

Traditional Pre-1978 Roles: Rural women of Afghanistan

As discussed in the previous sections, family is the single most important institution in Afghan society and motherhood happens to be the most sought after role of a woman. According to a survey conducted by Afghan Demographic Studies (ANDS) in 1975:69), only 1-2 % of either men or women reached the age bracket of 65 unmarried.[154] Afghanistan being a patriarchal society to its core, patriarchal attitudes governed life-crisis decisions such as the selection of the person, a woman wants to get married to. The honour and prestige of the family as well as its well-being rest on women of the family and they were considered to be the core of each family unit.

About 85% of the Afghan population live in rural areas. In comparison to their urban counterpart the women in the villages have enjoyed relative freedom of movement, in the sense they were allowed to move freely within the residential section of their villages because the villages were either totally kin-oriented or organized in kin-oriented segments.

Possessing more land in villages ensured more prestige in villages. The more affluent section in the villages lived in *qallah* or big dwellings like mansion. It had a big compound- a series of attached town houses with a shared mosque and several indoor and outdoor bathrooms, all surrounded by a wall. It was almost a village in itself. Hospitality or *mehmannawazi* has always been a very important part of Afghan existence and those who opened their homes to wayfarers (to people who are even unrelated) and family members enjoyed immense prestige. The guest house or *mehmankhana* or *hujra* (in Pashtun dominated areas) were extremely important component of the village household. The women in the houses used to do cooking and cleaning for the guests at the guesthouse. The lands initially were very cheap and those who had substantial land found themselves quite wealthy when the real estate values rose. Many Afghan men from wealthy backgrounds, during this period, did not use his wealth to acquire a new car or a new horse. Instead he used his money to acquire more wives and yet more land. All the wives used to live in the same household.

Women always wore small embroidered caps drapes with long scarves, normally bright red for young, white for widows.[155] The *Chadri*, a long, sack-like garment composed of a myriad of pleats cascading to the ground from a skull-cap, leaving only a crocheted window over the eyes, was seldom seen in a village according to Nancy Dupree. Only those few women, usually among the more well to do, who had been to big cities, who wore *chadri*, as a symbol of their sophistication.[156]

Under normal circumstances, Afghan rural women did not expend an inordinate amount of time or energy fetching water and collecting fuel. Social interactions used to take place between groups of women when they went to fetch water from rivers or spring. Fuel gathering was normally the chore of the younger sons who collected straw and scrub, while younger daughters collected dung along the village alleyways and pathways.[157] Both the girls and boys, sometimes very young in age performed the responsibility of taking the family animals to gaze.

Women worked with men in certain agricultural tasks such as harvesting of cotton, pulses, fruits and nuts. Nancy Dupree writes how melon harvesting was a greatly anticipated putting when the entire family moved from the village to camp on the hill side next to their melon fields. During the stay of the Duprees' in the rural areas of Afghanistan they had observed these practices and she wrote that these collective chores were typically carried out with much laughter and singing, in no way did they conform to the stereotype of women bound to unremitting labour.[158]The men and women in rural areas played complementary roles in some respect. Women in the villages enjoyed many interrelated work experiences with men. While the men harvested the grains and vegetables, the women processed them. The men herded and sheared the sheep, while the women spun wool. The men of household used to see the carpet at the markets which the women back home had woven. Dupree argues that mutual respect grew from the acknowledged interdependence of male and female roles and women derived self esteem and confidence from these cooperative efforts.[159]No monetary value was placed on women's labour.

Women in the Workforce

Women did not figure prominently in the statistics of individual who received payment for services or products in Afghanistan before the war. The first phase of the only national census ever taken was attempted as late as 1972, and the results indicate no more than general trends (Afghan Demographic Studies, 1975).[160] Furthermore, these figures were almost immediately questioned by a subsequent survey (World Bank, 1978).[161]

Several qualifications need to be kept in mind regarding the survey's finding that only 8% of women over the age of eight, in both rural and urban areas, were economically active, that is in a position to receive wages for their labour[162]. The housewives were excluded from this figure so were many other economic contributions to household and community. Among the rural section of the respondents, the samples of production related activities, including agriculture and animal husbandry, weavers and spinners represented the highest percent of women reporting earned income. The samples also indicated that women from the poorer families in the villages often worked as servants for the more affluent families. The managerial services which the rural women performed for example in training of young girls or management of the household in general were not mentioned in the report. The report was also silent about the role they played as the custodians of family finances and household supplies.

These women in rural part of Afghanistan, according to Nancy Dupree were typically matriarchs and were responsible for distributing harvest supplies in amounts calculated to last until the next harvest was brought in.[163] If she was inept, the family either starved or went into debt. Dupree observes from her personal experience of living in proximity of such women from 1962 to 1978 that these attributes misrepresent the stereotypes which characterise rural women as helpless, ignorant non-entities in Afghanistan.

According to both Central Statistics of 1976 and a survey by International Labour Organization conducted in 1978, more than 85 percent of the total number of workers in the field of handicraft were women. However most of the end products were never up for sale. The women embroidered, sewed or wove for their family members and never considered that their input can also fetch them economic reward. Most families considered it shameful to sell their handiwork.

Involvement is handicraft activities on an economic basis was, for the most part, a regional phenomenon. For instance, knotted carpet weaving and felt- making were more popular in the northern part of the country, including Herat. Flat woven carpets (gelim) were produced in the north also, but in large numbers around Ghazni and Hazarajat as well.[164] The Helmand and the Kandahar Province, on the other hand were more popular for the production of embroidery and beaded caps. Embroidered turban caps (kola) were mostly offered for sale in cities of the northern part though for most of the families, their family members only made it for them. During the 1960s and 1970s, an embroidered coat (postin) made of sheepskin became very popular in the West and these were made essentially in Kabul where Afghans and foreign entrepreneurs had set up workshops. Foreign designers set up thriving businesses by providing gelim-makers with modern, state-of-the-art designs. All these types of economic activities were primarily joint ventures where both men and women contributed. For example, the men were responsible for securing the raw materials and marketing of the finished product, while the women prepared the object that they were marketing. However, Nancy Dupree mentions that there must have been exceptions to this pattern and highlights that women sometimes took embroidered turban caps to market places in the north and also sold beaded caps and embroidered shirt pieces on the sidewalks of Kandahar.[165]

Most of the female workforces were found in cities and provincial urban centres, that too more specifically in Kabul. But the highest percent of female earners in these cities were professionals, technicians and administrators employed by the government, with a lesser percent in sales and production, or privately and self- employed. [166] These included shop owners, shop workers, household-based sellers, street vendors, knitter, tailors, embroiders, hair stylists, food and beverage producers running small, household-based factories.

Women in Agricultural Production in Rural Afghanistan

Afghanistan's pre-war economy was mainly based on agriculture and animal husbandry. The country has a low population density owing to a difficult topography and extreme temperatures and an arid to semi arid climate. In 1978, the last year of peace in Afghanistan, the country was self sufficient in food and was a significant exporter of agricultural product.[167] Manufacturing industry was generally underdeveloped, with the exception of a limited number of plants producing textile, medicines and cement.[168] The geo-strategic location of Afghanistan increased its importance and it gained international attention during the Cold War period. The superpower in order to have access to the vital position of the land provided significant quantities of foreign aid, which funded a centralised but relatively weak state structure, lacking any substantial domestic tax base. Foreign aid also funded a relatively good network of arterial road, providing transport corridors between the major cities and urban centres. Some major irrigation and hydro-electricity facilities, in addition to a number of (largely urban) health and educational programs were undertaken.[169]

In Afghanistan women involved in agricultural production are estimated at 65% of agricultural workforce.[170] Over the years the gender roles in agriculture has not experienced much change. Women carry out value-adding activities as domestic chores while trading and marketing of finished agricultural products are carried out almost exclusively by men, who are also the main financial beneficiaries of the process. Byravan argues two key factors contributing to these inequitable arrangements are gender biases based on deeply ingrained cultural norms and the highly informal agricultural economy.[171]

Afghanistan Research and evaluation Unit (AREU) conducted research on gender roles in agriculture for which it studies five villages in northern Afghanistan in 2004.[172] It showed that women in the studies villages were rarely considered for joint ownership of land and few females inherit land from their parents in practice, though Sharia law gives them property right. Thus, while unmarried and married women may have access to the produce from the land for consumption, they rarely own this very valuable asset. Where this appears to differ, however, is when a woman is widowed. It appears that in all of the villages studied landed widows do have certain rights over the land. Several widows involved in the study were sharecropping out[173] their land, mostly to male relatives, and receiving what appeared to be the correct share of the crop. It did not appear that those women had full rights of ownership, however, they were not permitted to sell the land, as it would be passed onto their sons or male relatives.

The majority of landowning males worked on the land, at least at harvest time. Men can be involved in all agricultural activities, whilst women from landowning households, widely considered to be wealthier households, appeared to have much less activity on land. This differed from village to village, however, based on age, assets owned and other activities being undertaken within the household. One of the richer women of one of the villages where study was carried out said that only poor women work on the land and that women are generally not allowed to work on the land "because of culture."[174] Where women from landowning households were involved in agriculture, it is limited to certain activities. Women from households who were sharecropping tended to work more with the men in their households on land. The sale of agricultural (or any other) produce is mostly the domain of men. No women, except for elderly widows (usually those who have no male children), travelled to the bazaar to sell or buy goods, which implied that it may be more difficult for women to make decisions over how money is spent.

In most of the villages across Afghanistan, there are households with a member or members sharecropping on another person's land, though to differing degrees.[175] Though women work with male household members in some aspects of sharecropping, all of the sharecroppers are generally male. Farming experience and expertise is needed to gain work as a sharecropper, and women who perform restricted agricultural activities do not acquire that expertise.

Another very important aspect of village economy is animal husbandry. Inside a household's compound in the village, women often take care of livestock such as sheep, feeding and watering them. Only a few women own live stocks like chicken and some sell the eggs to other women inside the villages. In some parts of Afghanistan, temporary migration takes place during the spring to other regions in search of greener pastures. Though there is no uniform role that Afghan women play under such situations, but from the survey that was carried out by Afghanistan Research and evaluation Unit (AREU) indicated that, both men and women migrated together to the pasture site. However there have been cases when only older women of the household were seen accompanying the men while the younger ones would stay back and devote themselves to carpet weaving. Women are responsible for making the tent-like structures that form the household's shelter during the time spent on the pasture.

Very few people in Afghanistan were restricted to farm labour only. Instead people did farm labour at certain times of the year and non-farm labour at other times. Some elderly women, and in particular elderly widows from landless households, used to work in melon fields during the spring as farm labour in return for one-seventh of the crop[176]. Some elderly women from landless households were also working in the orchards of others, guarding and picking the fruits.

It appears that gender roles in Afghanistan have been shaped by socio-cultural factors such as restricted mobility outside the village for many women, their often restricted ability to work outside the compound — partly brought about by women's role as the keepers of family honour — as well as the lack of ownership of the majority of productive assets by most women. These factors differ both within and across households depending on several dynamics. These dynamics include age, wealth and type of assets, social stigmas and economic returns attached to particular activities for certain groups of people, as well as household composition in terms of the number, age and sex of people available for different kinds of labour. No matter how vital a woman's economic contribution to her family's well being, this has remained secondary importance to her position as wife and mother. On marrying, a woman moves into the home of her husband, there exists a very strong Afghan code of honour which dictates that, once married an Afghan man must protect and care for his wife, her status increases significantly once she produces children, whilst childlessness for both men and women alike has been regarded as a calamity.[177] These patterns of participation in agricultural activities by women as well as their socio-economic standing got a huge blow when they were forced to leave their villages and take refuge in neighbouring countries like Pakistan and Iran.

Post 1978 Period: Refugee Experience of Afghan Women

The first type of migration was a massive and forced exile of mostly rural Afghans to neighbouring countries, Pakistan and Iran. This migration was directly related to the Soviet intervention in 1979 and its peak in mid 1980s. The exile still continued between 1985 and the beginning of the 1990s, but during the same period more than 1.5 million Afghans returned. The second half of 1990s brought extreme drought that forced thousands of Afghans to flee their homes in search of food and water. The Afghans remaining in Pakistan and Iran, originated primarily from rural areas, where they were small farmers, village artisans and tenants, or lower middle-class shopkeepers, civil servants and bazaar craftsmen.[178] Some of the middle-class people managed to continue their journey to industrialised countries. Around 70% of Afghans that sought refuge in Pakistan were ethnic Pashtuns of rural origin and a majority of the 1.2 million Afghan refugees living in Pakistan lived in refugee villages in North West Frontier Province, Baluchistan and Punjab.[179] Three quarters of them were women and children.

This turned out to be one of the saddest chapter in Afghanistan's long history even though Nancy Dupree feels that the successes of the refugee programmes have been remarkable: there have been no epidemics, little acute malnutrition and no real major outbreak of violence. Yet they had to live under extremely physical hardship.

In 1988 Dupree writes that "women (in the refugee camps), have endured physical difficulties with admirable fortitude. Now, however, after ten years of life in exile numbers of psychological and physical disorders have surfaced which will certainly affect the lives of these women after the resolution of the Afghan issue."[180]

The challenges for urban refugees were a bit different. They were not entitled to refugee assistance and had consequently experienced economic hardships causing them to abominate incurring marriage expenses for their daughters. In the changed environment of refugee camps, educational facilities were poor. Young men opted for *Jihad* rather than schools, this was especially true for the Afghan population in the Pakistan. Pakistan was facing tremendous crisis in the form of over flow of Afghan refugees since the Soviet intervention. In course of 1980s and 1990s the huge Afghan refugee population, predominantly Pashtuns, had started transforming the demographic characteristics of two frontier provinces of Pakistan- Khyber Pakhtunkhwah and Baluchistan, and also Federally Administered Tribal Areas (FATA). This allowed Pashtu to overwhelm other languages including 'Hindku', which was the language in use prior to this development. Original inhabitants of these regions now started moving towards bigger cities like Karachi and Lahore, forcing the Pakistani establishment to devise a policy that would unsure repatriation of these Afghan refugees and would reduce pressure on Pakistan. The policy they adopted to address the crisis included training of the young Afghans in the refugee camps to undertake *Jihad*.

Generations of Afghans were encouraged to choose *Jihad* over education in schools which resulted in the paucity of eligible educated men, further depleting the chances of marriages among urban educated families. Many urban educated refugee girls, preferred not to get married as they refused to be second wives or did not want to be with old and uneducated men. In addition to seeking employment to relieve the economic burden on their families, these women looked for meaningful activities to bolster self-confidence and self esteem. This trend was especially visible among women who migrated to western countries.

Conflict, War, Jihad: Change in the Demographic Balance

The Soviet intervention of Afghanistan, at the end of 1979 was the starting point of more than two decades of war that displaced more than one third of the Afghan population. Possibly nearly a million men have died fighting in the *jihad,* although accurate figures are impossible to obtain. Tens and thousands of widows were the direct fall out of such destruction. Thousands of young girls on the other hand lost their intended mates. Tradition dictated these women be provided for by male kin, but the presence of so many unattached women, many of whom with children, constituted economic burden, which in many cases became acute and effected the wellbeing of many women.

This resulted in multiple marriages. The institution of multiple marriages in Islam was encouraged after similar great battles fought during the time of Prophet Mohammed left countless women and children without sustenance and protection.[181] Also, the customary practice of the leverite, expressly forbidden in the Koran, whereby a widow was forced to marry her decreased husband's brother, seemed to be on the rise after years of declining popularity. Other widows married much older men reluctantly in order to provide for their children.[182]

Another disturbing development that took place was the apparent breakdown of conventional procedures for securing honourable mates for the girls. Although discriminatory practices of marrying of girls to pay off debts or acquire political or social advantages were not unknown in the past, preferred marriage partners had been first cousins, and in general, elaborate rituals associated with selecting mates were definitely mindful of the future happiness and the well being of the bride to be. Generally women were responsible for assessing the age and character of the groom as well as the acceptability of his family. Women drove hard bargain from the best financial arrangement to ensure respect and status for the bride, all these responsibilities added to her status within the family and throughout women's network and community.[183]

Since the withdrawal of Russians in 1989, Afghanistan has not been able to achieve peace and security. After every political conquest and transition of power from one group to another, waves of Afghans have fled the country to avoid persecution. The socio-cultural networks that was in place in Afghanistan prior to the population displacement was largely broken when they went to other countries. By that time too many first cousins had been killed and several marriages were contracted hastily by males for less than palatable circumstances.

Imposition of Stricter Behavioural Codes

All cultures tend to place greater protective restrictions when they encounter threat and at the various refugee camps this 'threat' perception resulted in the imposition of more rigorous behavioural codes. In the new environment of refugee camps the rural women were mostly confined to their homes (be it tent of mud hut). These congested camps tended to mix ethnic and tribal groups indiscriminately and there almost all had learned to wear *chadri.*

The urban families who believed in an equitable place for women were intimidated by the ultra conservative attitudes which insisted that women belonged to homes. Men stopped taking their female counter parts to public functions. Western dress, which at one point of time symbolised emancipation for women had become anathema and has been exchanged for local fashions which included closely wrapped *chader (*head shawls), leaving only the eyes visible, wrote Nancy Dupree, who did extensive work on the Afghan refugees in Peshawar, Pakistan. She further described that "heads had to be covered all the time in mixed company, inside or outside the home. Although this was galling to many men, as well as women, they acquiesced because to do otherwise would compromise the reputation of the women."[184]

Young girls from Kabul, so far brought up to take an education and choice of careers for granted, suddenly found themselves confined in strict seclusion and denied freedom of movement and opportunities to prepare for careers.[185] Professional women were forced to sit at home, or risked malignment if they sought employment with refugee organizations, such as hospitals, schools and welfare programmes. Dupree writes in the early years between 1978 and 1984, only courageous dared defy the conservatives who harassed them at work and passed poison-pen letters to their families.[186] Only those with male support persevered. The family, formerly seen by many as an oppressive restrictive institution, now became a bulwark for a modicum of freedom.[187]

Changing Attitude Towards Work

Attitude towards women's work also changed considerably. Gainful extra domestic activities for women were generally looked upon with disfavour in the past, except among a small section of population. Economic distress, idleness and boredom in refugee camps brought about changes in this attitude.[188] Many women who did not work earlier started generating a major portion of the family income. Male persistence often initiated their participation. Dupree cites an example of a charismatic lady nurse, who said "When there is no food on the table, men quickly open the door" to argue that when men were unable to find jobs, their insistence on *purdah* became less rigid.

Some women even adjusted to being principle wage earners, either because they were widows or their husbands were totally disabled to work after war wounds, or men in cases when the men in the family were incapable to find jobs. This trend was visible among rural women as well. They participated in income-generating and skill development programmes which were refugee oriented at large, such as tailoring projects producing quilts, school uniforms, books and bags.[189] Those who could do embroidery produced pieces which were stitched with the finished products like cloths and bags which the other women were making. Educated women from urban cities, assisted in the administration of these projects. Others taught or did administrative jobs in schools, or worked as nurses in hospitals and also taught English in English language classes. The obstetrics and gynaecological hospitals were staffed entirely with Afghan women professionals who also served at several mobile clinics.[190] Many others administered social welfare programmes for widows and orphans, making weekly trips into the refugee camps to identify and register needy cases.[191] These instances proved that when the need is there and the services are properly structured, women have taken the required initiatives and became independent. While the women in the refugee camps where struggling to adopt to the changed environment the situation back home turned grimmer.

Political Turmoil in Afghanistan and the Emergence of Taliban

The situation in the post-Soviet withdrawal era was witness to the death and injuries of Afghans and the destruction in Afghanistan in the first four months of 1994 was considered to be worst that what the country had suffered during the years of

Soviet occupation.[192] The situation further deteriorated when President Rabbani refused to step down, going against the previous deal between Mujahideen leaders who had decide to rule the country in turns. With Rabbanis' refusal, Gulbuddin Hekmatyar's determination to see him go led to further intensification of the bloodshed. The UN Special Mission also failed to bring the warring factions to negotiating table in September 1994. As a result, the Mujahidin leaders had demonstrated a disquieting low level of their commitment to peace and the well being of the civilians who lived in a constant state of fear and suffering.[193] They continued injuring a nation that already had suffered so much for their personal, ideological and ethnic ambitions and paved way for yet another dreadful era, the Taliban era.

The Taliban Phenomenon: Experiences of Afghan Women

The emergence of the Taliban marked a new phase in Afghan politics. Ahmed Rashid describes the Taliban as dangerous to ignore. Their interpretation of Islam has elements of black humour regarding human rights he said. They received support from only three countries, namely Saudi Arabia, Pakistan and United Arab Emirates. While much of the Afghan population suffered under the Taliban, women bore specific, unrelenting and often violent adversity, including denial of basic human rights, seclusion and segregation.

After taking control of the capital city of Kabul on September 26, 1996, the Taliban issued edicts forbidding women to work outside the home, attend school, or to leave their homes unless accompanied by a husband, father, brother, or son. In public, women must be covered from head to toe in a *burqa,* a body-length covering with only a mesh opening to see and breathe through. Women are not permitted to wear white (the colour of the Taliban flag) socks or white shoes, or shoes that make noise while they are walking. Also, houses and buildings in public view must have their windows painted over if females are present in these places. Furthermore, in January 1997, Taliban officials announced a policy of segregating men and women into separate hospitals.[194] This regulation was not strictly enforced until September 1997 when the Ministry of Public Health ordered all hospitals in Kabul to suspend medical services to the city's half million women at all but one, poorly-equipped hospital for women.[195] Female medical workers also were banned from working in Kabul's 22 hospitals. The Taliban's edicts restricting women's rights have had a disastrous impact on Afghan women and girls' access to education, as well as health care. One of the first edicts issued by the regime when it rose to power was to prohibit girls and women from attending school. Humanitarian groups initiated projects to replace through philanthropy what prior governments had afforded as a right to both sexes. Hundreds of girl's schools were established in private homes and thousands of women and girls were taught to sew and weave.[196]

On June 16, 1998, the Taliban ordered the closing of more than 100 privately funded schools where thousands of young women and girls were receiving training in skills that would have helped them support their families. The Taliban issued new rules for nongovernmental organizations providing the schooling: education must be limited to girls up to the age of eight, and restricted to the *Qur'an.*[197] Taliban policies that restricted women's rights and denied basic needs were often brutally and arbitrary enforced by the "religious police" (Department for the Propagation of Virtue and the Suppression of Vice) usually in the form of summary, public beatings.[198] The presence of Osama bin Laden, hosted by the Taliban, and his usage of Afghan territory for training Islamic militants for so called Islamic struggle across the world drew international criticism. But before September 2001, the aspect about Taliban rule which shook the world the most was the barbaric treatment of women and the gross violation of Human Rights in Afghanistan. Inspite of severe international criticism, Taliban leadership neither altered their modus operandi nor did they agree to part with their guest Osama Bin Laden. Human rights violation, ill-treatment of minorities, population displacement compounded with strict enforcement of the Shariat, poor administration, rise of militancy, existence of war economy with drug peddling, smuggling and arm trade marked the dismal state of affairs during the Taliban rule.[199] Women and girls were not allowed to come outside their homes without wearing *burqa.* Instances of lashing on streets and public humiliation of women were common. Women were whipped in public for revealing their ankle or part of their hair.[200] Bismillah Jan, an old *burqa* seller at out of the old markets of Kabul, though admits that his business suffered considerably after fall of Taliban, yet he expressed "I would never want them to come back and rule this country, if not for anything else, for my daughters."[201]The Taliban restrictions denied women of some of their most basic fundamental rights and therefore drew massive criticism from international community. Though many uncertainities throughout the Afghan history and restrictions were imposed by regimes like that of the Taliban there were certain institutions which prevailed-one such is the institution of marriage. The institution of marriage is centre to Afghan social life- regardless of region, ethnicity of kinship. There were many ways in which marriages were decided and practiced in Afghan families. The following section reviews that while emphacising on the concept of 'Bride price'.

Gender , Generation and Status: Marriage Practices in Afghanistan

A research[202] conducted by Afghanistan Research and Evaluation Unit in 2006 across Afghanistan indicated that, women have played a significant role in decision making pertaining to marriages in the family. A middle aged women from Herat city, interviewed in the study expressed that:

> "In buying things and building house, they (men) dont ask us and they dont listen to our ideas and wishes, but for children's marriages a mother has the right to give her opinion."

A man in his 50s from Bamyan province seconded her ideas saying :

> "Yes they participate in decision making and they should participate so that there wont be any conflict at home."

However this two statements mentioned above do not suggest that all women are in a position to exercise similar rights and influence across Afghanistan in the matter.The degree of influence that a woman has changes throughout her own and the wider family's life course. A woman who may have found it difficult to influence decisions at an earlier stage in her life usually gains more authority as she becomes older, particularly if she is widowed and perhaps also the oldest person in the family. In this case she may even become the primary decision-maker regarding the marriages of her children and grandchildren.

It was reported by several men interviewed in the study that their mother or *nasaka* mother (father's wife but not biological mother) had made the decision about their marriage.[203] Under other family circumstances and household structures, women who are younger can also be influential. Women's influence in decision-making can increase over the course of a family's life cycle as the men in the family come to rely on the advice of their wives. Islam permits men to possess more than one wife therefore it is common to find that wives of an Afghan man coexisting in the same house.

Though it is difficult to draw conclusions on many issues based on comparisons between the different provinces where the research was conducted by AREU. Nevertheless, while women across all the provinces play some role in scrutinising prospective spouses' families, it appears that women in Bamyan play a greater role in this than in the other provinces. This is likely to be related to the higher degree of mobility that Hazara women have, due to less rigid norms of sex segregation and women's seclusion in these communities than in those of other parts of Afghanistan.[204]

A significant amount of attention is often paid to the notion of forced marriage in Afghanistan . The archetypical notion of a forced marriage and the image that the expression "forced marriage" conjures in the imaginations of many is of a young girl being forced into a marriage, usually to a much older man. Girls and women, boys and men are sometimes made to marry against their wishes, which often have detrimental consequences for both them and the women they are forced to marry. A family may also be forced by another family to marry a child against their will. Cultural norms often force individuals to marry their children in a manner that is contrary to their personal desires. Such examples became more evident for the women from Afghan refugee communities, especially living in western societies. The daughters who were exposed to education and less stricter cultures of the host societies often didnot approve of their families choice of groom, who tend to look for proposal within their own community and even wanted their daughers to go back to Afghanistan after marriage. Despite there being a commonly held opinion in the communities that children should concent to their marriage, it was found that asking children for consent —particularly, but not limited to, the case of girls — was often done as a mere formality. "We have this custom that whatever parents do,their sons and daughters must approve of it, even if they do not consent in their hearts,"expressed a yound man from bamyan province.[205]

The bride price (*galah*) varies, depending on the status of the family, as well as the province, with necessarily no corealtion to the qualities of the girl. The relatively poor Pahtun dominated south-eastern border provinces, particularly Paktia, apparently has the highest brideprice.[206] Any relaxation in the sum by the bride's family, who have the final say is seen as lowering social standing of the family in the community and bringing disrepute to the bride.[207] In the post Taliban phase like most of other commidities in the country the bride price also has soared up according to some of the contemporary Afghan men in Kabul. As a young professional in his late 20s said, "in Pashtun dominated provinces the bride price range from US $ 15,000 to 25,000. By the way this price is not dependent on the beauty or education of the prospective bride...it is just a socio-cultural practice."[208] Though there are instances of love marriages however those are the exceptional cases. As expressed by one gentleman in Kabul, men feel that "if a girl can date another man before marriages, then she is not a wife material", [209] however for obvious reasons this rule is not applicable for men.

Various theories are advanced for the custom of bride price. While it is generally believed that the price is a sum paid to "buy"the girl into her husbands's family, who will then take on the responsibility of provinding for her for life. There are also certain sections of the society that advances the notion that the price is expected to compensate for the loss of revenue that will occour to the girls family in terms of productive household work, in relaesing her to the other family unit. Apart from the bride price the groom is expected to pay *meher* price, a sum that will definitely have to be paid in case he decides to divorce his wife, but will be rendered inapplicable if the women divorces him.[210] The final sum is setteled depending on the negotiations at the time of the marriage (*nikah)* itslef. Besides that, the bridegroom will also be responsible for all the wedding expanses, including the wedding feast (in two separate sections, split for men and women); bridal dress/ dresses. In the unban centres like Kabul brides generally wear two dresses, a green coloured one for the day of nikah ceremony and a white dress for the reception. The cost for bride's trip to beauty salon, gold jewellary, engagement of the officiating mullah; as well as the musicians and the team of vedio and cameramen are all payed by the groom's side. During the Taliban era, wedding extravagence was banned, But with their ouster the wedding industry has boomed, pushing many bridegrooms to years to debt. In the complex, custom-bound debate, one can be left throughly perplexed wondering that if the women in Afghanistan are so expensive", then why were not they treater better? The following chapter looks into the state, society and the politics related to gender in Afghanistan upto the international intervention in 2001.

Chapter-III

THE AFGHAN STATE, SOCIETY AND GENDER POLITICS UP TO 2001

Moghadam noted that scholarship on Afghanistan "has emphasized geopolitics over gender politics and neglected the place of the women in the reform program of Democratic Republic of Afghanistan."[211] She notes that the political and cultural projects such as uncovering women educating girls, legislating *hejab,* requiring burqa and honouring women's family roles are highly gendered, and the government initiatives to modernize have resulted in tribal rebellions.[212] The most evident divisions are between the sexes, but there are role patterns within Afghanistan that are less patriarchal and more complementary, for example women have the bride price. As a state Afghanistan is weak because of its inability to realise goals or regulate social relations and use resources in determined way.[213]

Hafizullah Emadi, on the other hand believes that the condition of Afghan women is one of inferiority and are discriminated from the birth. Male child is preferred because he is the inheritor of property and carries forward the family name. Women are bought and sold and her virginity is a symbol of honour. It is absolutely essential for a woman to preserve her virginity until she is married. There have been instances when women were subjected to death by her family if they felt that there has been a departure from this practice. Women are subject to strict social traditions that forbid them to talk with strangers and that separate them from men at such events as funerals and in public transportation.[214] Women's involvement outside the home does not weaken the tradition that they are the heart of the family, because honour and status of the family rest with them who are controlled and protected by the men.[215]

Nancy Hatch Dupree writes that "Afghan society is consistent in its innate belief in male superiority, giving men the prerogative to determine the dos and don'ts for women. Few challenge this. The Taliban are reinforcing the patriarchal norms wrapped in the mantle of Islam.[216]

Haron Amin, Afghan diplomat, claimed that the treatment that women in Afghanistan during the past few decades, especially Taliban regime is "not Afghan". He goes on to say:

> "If you look at the history of Afghanistan, you see that Afghan women were never beaten publicly because there was always a very, very high degree of respect provided or given towards them. In the 1860s, Ayisha Durrani, a forward intellectual women poet, in fact, wrote on political issues. We had women like that. In the civil composition in a civil society in Afghanistan, women have always played a very important role. Throughout the 20th century, you had progressive movement or governments in Afghanistan that wanted to copy and move along with what was happening in the rest of the world."[217]

Afghan history demonstrates a few instances like Queen Gawhar Shad, who ruled from her throne in Herat, an empire from Tigris River to China, since her husband was weak and is believed to have continued for another ten years after his demise.[218] As discussed in Chapter one, survey of Afghan history would indicate at eras which had taken concrete steps to improve women's position, however today those phases are viewed as mare departures from the accepted order in which women of Afghanistan would remain subjugated. According to Louis Dupree, the ideals of Afghan society were expressed in the 1931 Constitution, but due to political structure, the ideals were not always enforceable. Article 9 of the Constitution says that all persons having Afghan citizenship are equal. Women are not specifically mentioned, but were presumed to have shared in the rights mentioned in Section III. Among those rights were prohibitions of imprisonment without due process, slavery, search of personal property without an order, confiscation of personal property and forced labour.[219] The Constitution also dictated compulsory primary education, the appeal of court decisions, and freedom of press. Dupree said that despite the provisions of 1931 Constitution, "all persons were not given equal treatment before the law, and women held a decidedly inferior position in afghan society."[220]

Between 1920s to 1963, customs brought objections against women unveiling in public and their freedom to move about. Amanullah's radical reforms were defeated because it faced severe opposition from tribal areas and the tribal leadership on the other hand felt particularly threatened by the state policies towards women empowerment. A group of reformist bureaucrats and technocratic elites, who were dismayed with Amanullah supported Habibullah and legitimised his leadership on the basis of Islam by publishing a newsparer, *Habib-al-Islam* (Friend of Islam).[221] This newspaper propagated conservative social and political agendas and appealed for public support. Habibullah's supporters in Kabul tried to expand the writ of the state and established contact with individuals in provinces who were unhappy with Amanullah's policies. On the other hand pro-Amanullah forces were socially and politically demoralized and failed to effectively fight Habibullah and his supporters. A tribal rebellion sealed Amanullah's tenure on the throne and paved way for Habibullah. In the nine months of Habibullah's rule, state treasury went bankrupt, trade came to stand still. Huge money was spent on expansion of military and distributed to the tribal chiefs who demanded financial reward in exchange of their loyalty and support. In addition to money, Habibullah knew that state's position against women's empowerment would ensure tribal support and accordingly girl schools were closed and female students who had gone abroad for educated were asked to return and polygamy was brought back in to law. Habibullah was overthrown by General Mohammad Nadir, who proclaimed himself as the king. Understanding that the popular sentiment was averse to modernization; he made Islam a state religion and decreed that women must wear veils. He closed schools for girls and not until the last two years (1932 to 1934) of his reign could girls attend schools; and then, these schools were for girls alone.[222]

Mohammad Zahir Shah who took the throne in 1934 and rule until 1973, was more cautious in his approach. He established separate schools for girls and employed women in professions considered appropriate, such as teaching and medical personnel.[223] Although women's colleges had existed since 1946, women were admitted to Kabul University in 1959.[224] After him, Mohammad Daoud became the president (1973 to 1978) and repeated the trend of taking drastic steps and thereby forbade child marriages, declared dowry to be the property of the wife, established a family court with woman judge and recruited women in police and armed forces.[225]

Daoud was impressed by Soviet Union's authoritarian style of governance and economic policies. One of his thrust areas involved project on freedom of women, and he encouraged female ruling family members and wives of senior government officials to spearhead the unveiling of women. They did this publicly in Kabul in 1959, during the anniversary of country's independence. Conservatives, traditionalists and clerics, vehemently denounced this movement, however it gained wide support among middleclass and intellectuals.[226] One very important aspect about Daoud's drive for women's emancipation is the significant role played by the infusion of external capital in the country's modernization initiatives. Eminent scholar Hafizullah Emadi points out that, foreign consumer items flooded the consumer market in Afghanistan during that time, and businessmen and merchants who needed consumers to purchase their imported products viewed women as potential consumers. Thus he augues that women emancipation was necessitated by economic imperatives and Daoud's government only facilitated the process.[227] Soon opposition to Daoud's policies began to grow as the elites aligned with the kind began to view Daoud's closeness with the Soviet Union with suspicion. While opposition became stronger, removing Daoud and replacing his regime with an elected government seemed a viable solution.

Moghadam believes that Afghanistan's religious and tribal forces strongly opposed change.[228] Civil law in 1977 abolished child marriage and set the legal marriage age to 16, but the law did not address the husband's right to unilaterally divorce.[229]

Haron Amin stresses the importance of comparing what happened in Afghanistan with what was happening in the rest of Middle East.

> "Afghanistan joined United Nations in 1946, at that time there were only about 55 countries that joined United Nations. The independence movements that were advocated

> by a lot of these powerful middle-western countries begot a lot of new nations which were infant nations. But at the time, Afghanistan was already existing, it was a state, and so many of the middle eastern societies, by far the Afghans, had shown or exhibited a crescendo in terms of the women's liberation movement. Women were there in all aspects of life, poets, writers, ministers and members of parliament, already under the 1964 Constitution."[230]

Louis Dupree has written that in 1957, women worked in Radio Stations, in factories and in other workplaces, accompanied their husbands to over sea posts, composed delegation to a conference of Asian women in Cylone and in 1958, women delegation represented Afghanistan at the United Nations.[231] Amin notes that in 1959, women in Afghanistan were learning driving. Daoud's steps helped in further emancipation of the women of Afghanistan. Dupree states that, for the first time, women delegates entered the controversy over the meaning of the term "Afghan" in the line in the 1964 Constitution. Proposal was forwarded that women should be specifically mentioned in the Constitution by women but after an assurance came from the Constitution Committee that the word "Afghan" included both the genders, the proposal was withdrawn. Dupree concluded that "the emphasis on legal equality of women is one of the more important aspects of the 1964 Constitution.[232] Regarding abolition of *purdah*, both Amin and Dupree have argued that it was a social, political and economic reform. They mentioned that because of this step potential labour force in the country increased by 50%. Although women got the right to vote by the 1964 elections and it was application across the country but the fact was that women voted only in the large urban centres. One of the four women elected to the Afghan House of Representatives in the 1960s, explained,

> "Two women were members of the Counselling Committee in charge of drafting the new Afghan constitution. Four others, myself included, became members of the Grand Assembly, which adopted the constitution that same year. The movement for women's emancipation in Afghanistan began long before the communist takeover."[233]

From 1963 to 1973, two women were in government: Kobra Narzaye, Minister of Public Health from 1965 to 1969 and Shafiqa Zaizyee, political advisor, 1972.[234] Four women were elected to the government as deputees in the parliament from 1965 to 1969: Dr. Anahita Ratebzad, Khadija Ahrari, Roqia Abubakr and Masuma Esmati Wardak. Two women were in Mishranu Jirgah: Homeira Seljuki and Aziza Gardizi. Most women who participated in government were urban.[235]

The organized women's movement in 1964 consisted of two political groups, Feminists and Socialists. The Feminists advocated equality of men and women regardless of class and ideology, while the Socialists wanted to change the material bases of women oppression, the semi feudal and capitalist relations of production.[236] In 1968, when few conservative members of Parliament raised objection on women going abroad for education, hundreds of women gathered and protested against that. They pointed at the Constitution and showed that it guarantees equal right to men and women. Conservatives saw the rising awareness of women as anti-Islam and acid attack was carried out on several women by one of the religious leaders.

Article 31 and 32 Constitution also permitted formation of political groups and organizations and as a result quite a few political parties were formed espousing different agendas and political ideologies. *Sazman-e-Jawanan-e-Muttaraqi* (Progressive Youth Organization), *Afghan Millat* (Afghan Nation), *Sazmane-e-Jawanan-e-Musalman* (Islamnic Youth Organization), *Wahdat-e Milli* (National Unity), *Hizb-e- Muttaraqi-e-Democrat-e- Afghanistan* (Progressive Democratic Party of Afghanistan) and *Hizb-e Democratik-e-Khalaq-e Afghanistan* (People's Democratic Party of Afghanistan). People's Democratic Party of Afghanistan (PDPA) was headed by Noor Mohammad Taraki and was influenced by the Russian imperial state. Russian Intelligence Agency KGB recruited two agents, one of which was Taraki and the other one was Babrak Karmal and they recruited several other agents under them. The KGB financed the publication of PDPA's paper *khalq* (Masses)in 1966.[237] After repeated fallouts between these two prominent members of PDPA, Karmal left the party and formed his own party, *Parcham* (Banner). Both *Khalq* and *Parcham* retained the original nomenclature of the PDPA.

By 1978, the leftist group was in power and though they promised complete equality of men and women in reality that did not happen. Many like Sulima (who story has been narrated in the book *Behind the Burqa*), a girl in her teens during that time was overjoyed as she felt it was that best thing that could have happened to Afghanistan but within a short period of time she realised that there was a major price tag to be paid for the Communism that Afghanistan were importing.[238] President Daoud was overthrown in 1978 and Afghanistan became a democratic country. Nur Muhammad Taraki, the Secretary General of the Khalq faction of PDPA held the posts of the President, Prime Minister and the Chairman of Revolutionary Council. Taraki believed women belonged to the home and counted none as his follower.[239] Babrak Karmal, leader of the *Parcham* faction became the Vice-Chairman and Deputy Prime Minister, but for a short while only as within few months members of *Parcham* were removed from the cabinet. But they were forced to unite under Russian pressure in 1979.

The Social and Economic Impact of 23 years of War on Afghan Women

The Communist Regime (1979-1989)

During the period of Soviet military occupation, a central feature of government policy was the emphasis on education and vocational training including women's education. It is estimated that by the end of this period, women were to be found in all major government department, in addition to the police force, the army, business and industry.[240] They taught, studied and acted as judges in Family Court, dealing with issues relating to divorce, custody of children and other family matters. In urban areas they were seen performing roles of scientists and pharmacists in government laboratories and comprised over 75% of teachers, 40% of medical doctors and approximately 50% of civil servants.[241]

After President Taraki's accidental death, Hafisullah Amin was the new President. Once he came to power he tried to normalize relations with United States which for obvious reasons was not liked my Soviet Union and they eliminated and replaced him with Babrak Karmal. With this development, more women were employed in industry and social services because men were enlisted to fight. The Khalq Organization of Afghan Women (KOAW) was renamed the Women's

Democratic Organization of Afghanistan (WDOA), which was the only women's group that supported the Russian Invasion.[242] Women and men were declared equal "in all social, economic, political, cultural and civil aspects."[243]

Again women were called to support the nation and the "Glorious 27 December Uprising" On1st January 1980 Karmal issued a "Message to Oppressed Women and Mother of the Homeland" in which he noted:

> "our heroic women sometimes fought foreign invaders... with spears and pick axes... and with their pride and chastity supplied water to *ghazis* (heros) on the battlefield, and at other times hit the enemy passing through the streets with rocks and clods of earth... it is the duty of the revolutionary government of Afghanistan to guarantee the rights and the freedom of women in all social, political, cultural and other spheres of life. Women of Afghanistan, defend the dignity and honour of your homeland."[244]

The verbal attacks on Amin's excessive repressions were even more venomous than those previously dictated against the defunct "feudal". All the attacks were vehement, but the most vitriolic denouncements came from Dr. Anahita who upheld the tradition that Afghan woman incapable when aroused. She characterized Amin as a "cruel and criminal murderer with a fraudulent devil's soul," "a savage despot with ruthless fascistic manners", "a beasty lunatic", guilty of "savage acts of looting killing and outraging the honour of the suffering and noble people of Afghanistan in order to keep his throne"[245]- and much, much more. Her phrases were less elegant than those of past poet-heroines, but they were certainly rousing.

The resistance to the communist regime became focussed increasingly in the rural areas, an estimated 5 million people fled from the countryside as refugees to Pakistan, Iran or further a-field.[246] Much of the destruction that occurred during this period resulted from Soviet bombing of those rural areas harbouring resistance to the Kabul government. However some of it was directly attributable to the contested place that education (women's education in particular) had come to assume within the wider political and philosophical landscape of the conflict.[247]

The Decree Number 7 issued during this time, forbade forced marriages and required minimum age to marry, with an imprisonment penalty. Rosemarie Skaine, cites in her book that according to Online Centre for Afghan Studies, this decree advocated the liberation of women but its agenda was a "direct and open attack on Afghan culture and honour.[248] There were instances of the Communists using force if the villagers did not attend literacy classes. Some Afghan refugees in Pakistan also showed this to be their reason for fleeing their country.[249] Valentine Moghadam, has noted that compulsory education for girls, raised the threat of women refusing to obey and submit to male authority. The reason for objection to these were a product of male chauvinism on one hand, writes Moghadam, while the other argument was that education brought dishonour to the women and the household because they were not in Purdah, there were others who felt that this was too much of an intrusion by the State in their domestic lives. Forbidding the bride price, payment due from groom to bride either for her widowhood or to her father for lossof her labor, also prevented traditional transactions that ruined the economy of households that needed bride price as convertible capital in future. Goodwin writes, that five years into the Soviet occupation, the organization was still only offering six month literacy courses and needlework classes. The programme, he said was not as successful for its students and did not reach as many women as the propaganda claimed.[250]

Rosemarie Skaine quoted Morawarid (Mora) Hashimi and her brother, Rahman, in ther book, who fled to Pakistan in 1983 to escape Soviet oppression and then came to the United States. Rehman described life before the invasion to the author:

> "A normal life, you know. Everything was Ok. We weren't restricted. We were free. We could speak. We could speak with each other. We had free movement. Everything. The Russians came in, and we were restricted. As with the communist countries, you have heard a lot of stories about (Esat) Germany, of course. The same thing there, you know... Everything is under control, you know, no freedom, talking, nothing."

The protracted war against the Soviet occupation had a devastating impact on Afghanistan's economy and on the lives of rural women. The combined impact of large-scale exodus from the countryside, the destruction of traditional irrigation systems and lack of skilled expertise for their maintenance, and the widespread and indiscriminate laying of landmines, resulted in a sharp decrease of agricultural output, and depletion of livestock herds.[251] At the same time, what Government-provided social services were essentially restricted to urban centres.

Activists and scholars see Afghan women in struggle, but they see them also as a strong and as women of accomplishment. Catherine Daly says, "As in many countries cultures, it is women that really pass on the traditions. Afghan women, as most women, are very hard working individuals and they are very, very committed to their families, their children and their husbands."[252] According to Haron Aziz, many women helped to form the Mujahideen in 1979 and then later, again played a role to free the country from Soviets. In 1980, the Revolutionary Association of the Women of Afghanistan resisted Soviet occupation.. Hafizullah Emadi wrote, "Women's role in the national liberation struggle was not restricted to rallies, protest demonstrations, noncooperation with the enemy, etc. They participated in organized struggle such as abduction, assassination and bombing of enemy positions.[253]

The Mujahideen Period (1992-1996)

Personal and political differences over the future course of development between *Parcham* and *khalq* factions of pro-Soviet ruling party *Hizb –e-Watan (*formerly PDPA) and escalating armed struggle by US backed Islamic fundamentalists known as Mujahideen (Islamic warrior) led to the collapse of the Communist regime. If the period of Communist administration was characterised by displacement and devastation in the countryside but relatively peaceful conditions in the cities, the exact reverse was true for the period when the Mujahideen administration was in power. Khaled Hosseini in the bestseller *A Thousand Splendid Suns* captured the initial positive response that the Mujahideens generated among the people and the fighting that was taking place between the various factions were seen by some of the people as "temporary", as one of the characters in the book was optimistic and believed that this may stop and "they'll sit down and figure something out".[254] However as the situation worsened in Kabul, the story depicted that a man tried to convince his wife to leave Kabul (like many others), which has ceased to be a safe place by mid 1992. He believed that all these Mujahideens knew was war as "they learned to walk with a milk bottle in one hand and a gun on the other", however his wife was in awe with them. She snubbed her husband and shot back, "Did you fight Jihad? Did you abandon everything you had and risk your life? If not for the Mujahideen, we'd still be the Soviets' servants...and now you'd have us betray them!"[255] Since the Mujahideens were seen as the force that brought end to the era of foreign (Soviet) domination, the initial mood after the resignation of Dr. Najibullah was that of hope and celebration.

The sense of optimism that was among the people when they captured power was quickly dashed as internecine conflict erupted between the different factions. During this time the population displacements were mainly from the cities, especially Kabul. There was also significant number of internally displaced population within cities as the ethnic identity of certain neighbourhoods became more entrenched. During the Soviet period, Kabul was viewed as the epicentre of all the vices and the reason for country's misfortune, a view born out of country's political perspectives, but was related to different religious and cultural aspirations for Afghanistan's future, which included issues of women's rights. For the conservative rural-based Mujahideen opposition, Kabul and other cities were perceived to be centres of 'sin' and 'vice' precisely because of the high visibility of educated, emancipated, urban women.[256] There was a perception that population of Kabul, which was the most prosperous section of Afghan society during the Communist regime, was getting punished by the Mujahideen for their silent collaboration with the occupation and for the 'immoral values' propagated by the Communist regime. The city was reduced to rubbles.

The Islamic fundamentalists that were regarded by the West as freedom fighters in the 1980 engaged in the bloody civil war in the 1990s that led to the destruction of country's infrastructure and transformation of Afghanistan into wasteland. Warring factions seized men and women of rival groups as well as non combatant civilian hostages, and raped and mutilated their captives.[257] The mistreatment of their captives ranged from disfiguring their faces by gouging out eyes or cutting off ears and noses to locking them in metal containers, leaving them to die of starvation of dehydrated.[258] Armed confrontations among warring factions continued and so did efforts to make peace between them. None of these leaders managed to effectively build grassroot support and their policies never transcended tribalism and regionalism. This period witnessed bitter war that claimed lives of thousands of people pitting Shias against Sunnis and one ethnic group against another. Almost all factories and manufacturing facilities were destroyed, with the result that women and men who had been employed in such industries were left without alternative employment. Most government schools remained closed during this time (many were used to house people who were displaced from other parts of Afghanistan). With disproportionate impact on women who comprised a majority (70%) of trained teachers.[259] There were women pilots, women diplomats and women generals, Dupree says that women did have predominant roles in society.[260] Mavis Leno testified to the U.S Senate that

> "Before the Taliban gained dominance in Afghanistan, women were as crucial part of the workforce. In Kabul, for example: 70 percent of teachers were women; 40 percent of the doctors were women, over half the university students were women; schools at all levels were co-educational;

> Afghan women held jobs as lawyers, judges, engineers, and nurses; and Afghan women were not required to cover themselves with the burqa."

Government Ministries were also target of frequent shelling and rocket attacks, consequently even when ministry buildings remained open, families were often reluctant to allow their employed female family members to report for work.[261] However some women continued to work in the health facilities that were operational, in the offices/ programmes of the limited number of NGOs and international agencies that remained and in domestic industries such as carpet weaving and handicraft production.

Flight from the cities was mainly to camps established to receive IDPs, however where city dwellers were able to take refugee with relatives in the villages, this added to economic pressures on the countryside. Sultan Barakat and Gareth Wardell writes arterial roads were in control of different local commanders at this time, each of whom levied a "tax" on aid convoys, vehicles and even individual bus passengers.[262] A typical journey from Kabul to Jalalabad, or from Kabul to Mazar-e-Sharif (when the Salang highway was open) might entail negotiating access through over 45 check-posts wrote the author from his personal experience. Naturally, these conditions exercised a huge disruptive impact on trade, marketing products, the rural economy and the women and men working in that sector. Hafizullah Emadi writes that not a single ethnic group could claim it did not have a role in the destruction and murder of innocent people, all were equally responsible for the war and the violation of human rights, although many intellectuals tried to exonerate their own ethnic communities and blame others for the brutal war of ethnic cleansing.[263] Prominent radical organizations that denounced the brutal civil war included the Afghanistan Liberation Organization (ALO) and the Revolutionary Association of Women of Afghanistan (RAWA), publishing anti-war literature and organizing antiwar rallies and meeting in Pakistan and North America. The Mujahideens were eventually discredited and lost public support, leading to the emergence of Taliban, which also declared opposition to the war.

The Taliban Regime (1994-2001)

Within a very short period of time after their emergence on the Afghan military scene, the Taliban had taken control of over 80 percent of Afghanistan. As they consolidated their hold on power, so security improved in the cities, check-posts were removed from the roads and there was a general improvement in the economy. According to the World Bank, the economic recovery was concentrated mainly in the rural areas of the country that was taken over relatively early by Taliban. Barriers to trade were removed. Even in those areas, women continued to contribute in traditional ways to the functioning of the rural economy, particularly where they lived in large family groups.[264] However their policies towards the cities were starkly different.

In the cities, the Taliban social policies led to drastic curtailment of women's freedom to move, to be educated and to work. Restrictive policies were applied very strongly in most of the urban centres but most acutely in Kabul, Mazar-e-Sharif, Herat and other Dari speaking urban centres where women had traditionally enjoyed a greater degree of freedom that in the most conservative Pashtun heartland cities of Kandahar and Jalalabad.[265] This derived from their particular cultural interpretation of Islamic teaching, but also from the on-going war mentality writes Ahmed Rashid in his *Taliban, Islam, Oil and the New Great Game in Central Asia.* Taliban fighters were encouraged to bring "their" women with them to cities, as a mechanism for ensuring the morality of their troops; a policy that then resulted in much more conservative Pashtun practices being applied to urban women.[266] Eleheh Rostami-Povey quotes a women named Najia saying:

> "Even small minority of educated women and middle-class women were forced to marry the Taliban. I know of an educated woman who was the head of the school of medicine at the university and was forced to marry the Taliban. They were either forced or did it out of poverty or fear. Sometimes a woman who was married to one Taliban was raped by ten other Taliban. Sometimes they were taken outside of Afghanistan, especially to the Gulf region and were sold as sex workers."[267]

In the book *Behind the Burqa,* the Taliban were termed a s 'second generation Mijahideen'.[268] Many had originally been part of the Mujahideen forces. They were disturbed by the corruption and the un-Islamic behavior of their fellow soldiers and the leaders, felt one of the two women (Hala), whose story the book tried to depict. Some of them were passionate Afghan refugees, studying at madrassas in Pakistan. Most were orphans, who were clothed, fed and brainwashed at these religious schools and were raised to be fighters for God. These boys were brought up to do one thing: to fight for Islam and kill anyone they believed might stand in the way.[269]

It was not known what turned these Taliban leaders and their army of followers into people who hated women enough to institute the cruelest, most oppressive system against women ever to exist.[270] Some people thought this was because most of them were orphans who were brought up without the love of a woman. They were nurtured instead on the hatred taught by their version of Islam. It was ironic that the Taliban originally banded together as a group after some Mujahideen had kidnapped and raped a young girl. They believed that Mujahideen were degrading Islam and decided to avenge the honour of the violated girl and the honour of their violated religion.[271] But once they acquired power they became greatest violators of women.

Girls and women were denied opportunity to attend schools or receive education, although policies on these issues were subject to change and modification. It should be noted that the edicts relating to dress and appearance affected men as well as women; minority groups as well as majority. Initially they were closing down boys schools as well. They insisted that all men grow beard, or risk being beaten. Both government services and employment were denied to men without beards. The women were forced to wear not only Islamic *Hijab* or *Chaddari* but also *burqa*- a thick head- piece covering the entire head and the shoulders, with only a tiny rectangle mesh through which to see. Some of the elderly women believed Taliban could not be worse than the Mujahideen and they felt "at least they were protecting women by keeping them in the house, at least they were bringing order back."[272] In some ways women's situation was worse during the civil war that during Taliban rule. This was because so many women were murdered and raped by the Mujahideen. The Taliban disarmed the commanders and warlords and brutally enforced their own model of law and order. Eleheh Rostami-Povey quotes a women named Guita, who explained:

> "Sometimes they would beat women in the streets and nobody could do anything. People just stood and watched. They had a stick with lead at the end of it to beat women to cover themselves. It was difficult to see though the *chaddari*. When we went shopping we could not see what we were buying. If we put the *chaddari* up to see, they would hit us and close the shop. So shop keepers were not selling things to women."

Even privately organized schools at the homes were forbidden, although many such clandestine ventures existed. Batya Swift Yasgur shares the experience of one woman who was involved in such an initiative. She says that her school did not start as a way of defying the Taliban it just happened when one of her neighbor's daughter in Kabul started coming to her for guidance in her studies. Soon her siblings and other kids of the neighbourhood also started coming to her house for tuitions. With time the number of students multiplied, but all through the while they were extremely sacred and feared that they would get into terrible trouble for running a school. "We could be beaten. We could be killed"[273] , they felt if the secret was out.

Women were denied the freedom to work (other than health sector) and forbidden to leave their homes unless completely veiled and accompanied by a male relative. Following strong protests by the international community over the wholesale dismissal of female government employees after the Taliban captured power, it was agreed that they could continue to draw their salaries without being allowed to perform their work functions.[274] However, in 1999 the Report of the UN Secretary General on the situation of women and girls in Afghanistan noted reports of the widespread dismissal of female civil servants in a move to cut government spending.[275]The UN Special Rapporteur on Violence Against Women, who visited Afghanistan in 1999, noted that war-related physical abuse against women had decreased. However she found official, widespread and systematic violations of the human rights of Women in Afghanistan and in those areas controlled by the Taliban, it was noted that discrimination against women was officially sanctioned and pervaded every aspect of women's lives.[276]

Several edicts were issued attempting to regulate women's behaviour. For example they were forbidden from working in foreign agencies, assistance to widows a and needy[277] women could only be provided through their male relatives and without the employment of females; women could not be appointed as senior staff on foreign run hospitals; women were to walk calmly and avoid creating noise by their footsteps; they were forbidden to travel in a vehicle with foreigners. Batya Swift Yasgur's *Behind the Burqa,* depicts many horror stories. A lady depicts her experience at a market place where a woman wore a pant which was little short and her ankle was showing. Immediately, a turbaned, bearded Religious Police, wearing a white uniform seized her arm and pushed her against a wall- "*Hey Kafir*! Infidel! You are exposing your flesh!". He lashed at her with his whip as muffled cries came from beneath her burqa.[278]

Under the Taliban, thousands of female-headed households, who were internally displaced, lived in refugee camps around cities, most of their husbands having been killed during the civil war years and under Taliban rule. They were called *Zanane bee Sarparast* (unprotected women), a derogatory term.[279] A section of Refugee Centre in Kabul was reserved specifically for them where, separated from the other households, they lived as a separate community. Women, men and children suffered from malnutrition and various other diseases. Years of repression, deprivation and dire socio-economic conditions had severely affected the mental well-being of the majority of citizens. As Suraya Parlyka, head of National Union of Women of Afghanistan, explained: "We all suffered from the psychological pain of the war and destruction. It is going to take a long time to reduce and cure the pains of Afghan women, especially female headed households and the orphanages."[280]

While restrictive policies were applied in all Taliban controlled areas, the impact was most severe in Dari-speaking centres. However there were evidences that those organizations which, out of a concern that Afghan women continue to benefit from their programmes, chose to adopt more practical and non-confrontational approach to deal with the Taliban, were able to successfully negotiate a softening of some Taliban policies. The UN Special Advisor on Gender Issues and the Advancement of Women noted that during early 2000, the UN and the NGO assistance community were able to bring about a number of positive developments relating to employment of women such as, by mid- 2000 a total of 5,874 women were employed by the international assistance community in Afghanistan, despite Taliban restriction.[281] However additional restrictions were imposed later the same year. During the same time, the UN Special Rapporteur also visited areas which were not under the control of Taliban but the United Front. There she observed instances of female education taking place up to university level and where no official gender discrimination existed. However, she also noted that women in the regions which were under control of United Front also suffered from narrow access to education, health services and income generating employment.[282] In 1998, the executive director of Physicians for Human Rights, Leonard Rubenstein said, "We are not aware of any place in the world in recent history where women have so systematically been deprived of every opportunity to survive in the society- from working to getting an education to walking on street to getting health care."[283]

Inspite of these restrictions, women have bravely sought out substitute ways of surviving and devising their objectives within the context of their traditional and cultural practices. Though during this time the social capital eroded to a considerable extent in Afghanistan, however it must be admitted that both Afghan men and women relied upon social relations whenever they needed support. This was perhaps the most important asset through which they kept their families and communities together. They built the foundation for creating social capital which was essential for the process of reconstruction. Women worked together in groups and organizations, generating networks, norms and trust in their communities.[284] Even while passing through the toughest of times, women of Afghanistan had always hoped that the coming days would mark a departure from the trauma they had experienced. When Mujahideen captured power they were optimistic about their future and had hoped that those who have saved the country from foreign (Soviet) domination would do country for the country and the people. They were proved wrong. When the Taliban came to power they were again hopeful that they cannot possibly be worst that than the Mujhahideen. They were proved wrong. Describing the experience of women under Taliban, Afghan diplomat Haron Amin, had said that "they (Taliban) have not been able to provide women with any means of sustenance or any means of living, and so what you make out of this situation is neither Islamic nor Afghan."[285] RAWA compiled an “abbreviated” list of 29 restrictions ends on women and 11 restrictions applicable to All Afghans. The list ended with the words, “and so on…”, RAWA said that even if the number of rapes and killing fall, “Taliban restriction- comparable to those from the middle ages- will continue to kill the spirit of our people while depriving them of human existence.”[286]

The year 2001, provided yet another turning point for Afghan people in the backdrop of an unfortunate event that brought Afghanistan back to international glare. The September 11 incidents , the same year shook America to an extent that the administration within a month of the September 11th attacks, decided to deploy US Army in Central Asia to confront the terrorists on their own ground in the form of *Operation Enduring Freedom.* The Bonn Agreement drawn by the international community in the same year in order to achieve stability in Afghanistan , provided a blue print of the political, social and economic reconstruction designed by the international community brought forth several critical issues and dilemmas. Women's issues were among the most prominent ones.They were promised a better life in terms of peace security, Development, Democracy, Opportunity and Rights. They consolidated their role as social actors and they had great hopes that after the fall of Taliban their situation would improve. Slowly, after the fall of Taliban they began to challenge patriarchal gender relations. The process of ‘being heard’ was never meant to be easy and as expected was filled with stumbling blocks. How far their hopes and aspirations about improved lives and better future have been achieved, will be the matter of discussion in the following chapter.

Chapter-IV

AFGHAN WOMEN SINCE THE FALL OF THE TALIBAN

Afghan Women at the Start of Twentieth Century

Some years back when the world was celebrating the arrival of the twenty-first century, the part that Afghanistan played in the global festival was to present a dark, backward look, as if to another century—and nowhere darker than for the half of Afghanistan's people who are women.[300] Twelve years into the new century, Afghanistan has gone through another decade of upheaval, which has produced a mixed situation of progress and regress at the same time. Afghanistan in the year 2000 was a country with the world's largest number of displaced persons, its highest mortality rate, and its biggest production of opium. It was a country where more than half of its population was virtually invisible, totally ignored in its social, political, and economic spheres. Bonn Agreement in December 2001 opened a new phase in Afghan history.

Western media informed the world that Afghan women had been liberated, that they had thrown off their *burqas* and gone back to school.[301] The traditional Afghan 'burqa' became a symbol of oppression and pictures of women being beaten by the Taliban in public for offences were telecast all across the globe. On September 22 2001, CNN aired the documentary 'Beneath the Veil', which claimed an audience of five million Americans, building revulsion in their minds against *burqa*-clad women being beaten up. The documentary was aired several times on numerous channels, discussed in various talk shows and was perhaps one of the most watched documentary in CNN's history.[302] As discussed earlier, one of the primary factors leading to the rise of censure and disapproval of the Taliban was their treatment of women. The level of attention this issue managed to get was unparalleled. The media gave great attention to the issue as the number of articles on the theme rose dramatically by more than 30 times from August to November 2001. In fact, Afghanistan became a country where 'for the first time women's rights were used as a justification for international intervention.'[303]First lady Laura Bush claimed in a radio address on November 17, 2001, "The fight against terrorism is also a fight for the rights and dignity of women."[304]

In 2001, *Business Week* ran an issue that featured a photograph of an unveiled Afghan woman with the word 'liberation' printed above her.[305] The cover page declared, 'the US victory is a defining moment – for the Afghan people, for Western values, and for the cause of moderation in the Muslim world'. The article continued by arguing that the:

> . . . liberation of Afghanistan from the tyranny of the Taliban is a watershed event that could reverberate for years. The warm embrace by ordinary people of the freedom to do ordinary things is a major victory for Western humanist values. This victory of values, in the long run, may count for far more than the hunt for Osama bin Laden.

Time ran a special report on Afghan women on 3 December 2001. The cover had a picture of a woman without a veil and the caption read, 'Lifting the Veil'. The story began, predictably, by describing scenes of women shedding the burqa, which they refer to as the 'body bag for the living'.[306] However, the report took a cautious approach to the question of liberation, asserting that women were not going to be liberated overnight because 'Afghan society is tribal and conservative'.[307] Although the article questioned the future for women under the US backed Northern Alliance, it avoided any discussion of the US's role in fomenting the rise of Islamic fundamentalism in the region.

According to the *Communique* of RAWA on December 10, 2007, "The United States and its allies tried to legitimize their military occupation of Afghanistan under the banner of 'bringing freedom and democracy to the Afghan people." The same organization, in its March 2008 *Communique* stated, "After the United States and its allies invaded Afghanistan seven years ago, they misleadingly claimed to bring peace and democracy and to liberate Afghan women from the bleeding fetters of the Taliban...". The chief justice of Supreme Court, around the same time had publicly condemned equal education as "evil".[308] In Herat the warlord/governor Ismail Khan had forbidden men to teach girls, and the girls schools were closed. In Jalalabad, bombs had demolished two girls schools , and female teacher was murdered. News of girls being abducted from Kabul streets started to go around. A BBC report noted, "... Western journalists and aid workers who thought that piles of *burqas* would be burned in the street as the Taliban made a quick getaway are in shock. They are incredulous that what has been perceived as the arch symbol of Taliban rule is worn even when the regime in long gone."[309]- an indication of the ignorance of the realities of Afghan culture by people who were entrusted responsibility of bringing 'change'. Within a few years, any optimism that Afghanistan might have been entering a new era of peace, security and development appeared to be questionable. Shinkai Karokhail, Member of the Parliament of Afghanistan expressed

> "After the fall of the Taliban everyone wanted to come and work for women's rights, they were proud to say they were here to help Afghan women. Slowly, slowly this disappeared. Maybe the international community saw that we had two or three women in the cabinet, and thought, it's ok, now they have their rights. But we have lost everything, from those cabinet positions to the donor attention. Women are not a priority for our own government or the international community. We've been forgotten."[310]

The United Nations Development Programme (UNDP)[311] and the World Bank[312] argued that reconstruction and development were urgently needed, otherwise the country is likely to slip back into chaos and abject of poverty. By 2007, 39 percent of the population in urban areas and 69 percent of the population in rural areas do not have access to clean water. One out of eight children died because of contaminated water, life expectancy was forty four. 53 percent of the total population live below the poverty line, adult literacy rate was 29 percent and in some areas less than 1 percent of the population was literate. Very little had been invested in reconstruction. Out of 21,000 kilometres of roads, only 2, 793 kilometres were paved. There were forty seven airports in the country, but only ten had a proper runway.[313] Women continued to be victims of the state that directed its attention towards militarization rather that housing, health, education, infrastructure and welfare.[314] However it would erroneous to imagine that no attempts were made to improve the plight of women.

Changes brought into the Lives of Afghan Women

For all its short comings, Bonn Agreement turned out to have some very substantial provisions on issues of women's political participation, human rights, and transitional justice. It also pledged to address the structural impediments to women's rights in Afghanistan and to include women in political life. Important measures by the government include the allotment of 25% seats for women in the lower house of the parliament (Wolesi Jirga), and 17% women's seats in the upper house (Meshrano Jirga). Furthermore, the October 2004 elections showed a massive turnout of women voters. Interestingly, although women comprise 40% of the electorate, the number of women voters outnumbered that of men.[315] Significant steps like Afghanistan Independent Human Rights Commission (AIHRC) and of state machinery—what became the Ministry of Women's Affairs (MoWA)—to deal with huge imbalances in the field of women's rights and their position in the society due to the restrictions and violations of their rights during the years of war, were established.[316] The mandate of the MOWA as stated in their official documents was

> *"to support the government in its response to the needs and issues affecting women in all sectors of life in order to attain gender equality and full enjoyment of women's human rights; to ensure Afghan women's legal, economic, social, political and civic rights- including their rights to be free from all forms of violence and discrimination- are respected, promoted and fulfilled."*

The Gender and Law Working group, a women's lobby, was able to push through some amendments to the draft constitution released in 2003. These amendments, retained in the final document and approved in 2004, included an explicit reference to the equality of men and women before the law (Article 22) and increased the number of women in the legislature's lower house to two female delegates from each province (Article 83).[317] How effective MOWA, has become as part of the larger power sharing business over the past ten years, is a separate issue; for most Afghan women who worked actively at the grassroots level, and for the NGO community more broadly, simply having such mechanisms at the national level has been a major achievement.

One of the successes of the MoWA has been its provincial departments, which in a number of places have proved more effective than the central offices in Kabul in advancing women's interests locally.[318] Women who run these departments in different provinces have remarkable stories of how challenging it has been for them to start their work, and how they have become a destination for women who have experienced domestic violence or for families who have had disputes among themselves. Often, the women at the provincial level mediate among the families and solve the conflicts. It is important to mention that institutions at subnational level as such are crucial mechanisms to be used for peace-building and reconciliation processes, given their expertise and daily experiences with conflict resolution.

In 2003–04, in accordance with the Bonn Agreement, the interim president, Hamid Karzai, established an independent Constitution Review Commission that drafted a proposed new constitution for presentation to, review by, and then approval of a *Loya Jirgah* (Grand Assembly) of elected people's representatives.[319] At this drafting stage, the state minister and women's affairs minister jointly formed the Gender and Law Working Group (GLWG) with logistical support from the United Nations assistance mission in Afghanistan (UNAMA) and the UN Fund for Women (UNIFEM). The GLWG consisted of representatives from the Judicial Reform Commission, the Afghan Independent Human Rights Commission, the Supreme Court, the attorney general, the University Faculties of Law and *Shari'a,* and national women nongovernmental organizations—all Afghans, of course—as well as some international experts on gender and Islam. This group worked extensively on the draft and came up with specific recommendations for language in the constitution affirming equal rights of women and men, guaranteeing women's political participation, and acknowledging the state's obligations to implement various conventions and treaties that Afghanistan has signed or ratified.[320] The women's rights and human rights groups mostly used this platform of the GLWG for putting together their demands, as it was an informal group. Certain other significant developments in favour of women's rights in the country were:

- A landmark law was enacted – the 2009 Elimination of Violence against Women Law (EVAW)[321]
- A new National Action Plan for the Women of Afghanistan (NAPWA) received initial endorsement.[322]
- Women's shelters were established in Afghanistan for the first time.[323]
- 27% of the seats of Parliament of Afghanistan were reserved for women.[324]
- 25% of government jobs were reserved for women.[325]
- More than 2 million girls went to school.[326]
- More women were free to participate in public life and to work outside their homes as doctors, teachers, entrepreneurs and lawyers – a situation once made impossible by the Taliban.[327]
- Financial assistance and aids were available which were channelized for women's uplift projects and schemes.[328]

The Afghan media has developed considerably, and has helped highlight women's rights issues to certain extent. Radio transmission reached 65% of an overwhelmingly illiterate populace. Radio programmes help educate women, and a number of NGOs use radio to get their message across and educate women on important gender issues.[329] The US based NGO has been funding 18 radio stations in Afghanistan. Most radio stations have been broadcasting women's programmes on a daily basis. With funds from the United Nations Educational, Scientific and Cultural Organisation (UNESCO), the country's first women-operated FM station 'Voice of Afghan Women' started operating. According to Jane Mc Elhone, project director of an NGO IMPACS states: "For many Afghan women who still live very isolated lives, radio can serve as a bridge to the outside world. It can help them develop skills to survive in their daily lives. It can make them feel less alone."[330]

Role of International Community: Reform through State and International Law

The Bonn Agreement of 2001 proved to be instrumental in setting the agenda for women's rights in Afghanistan under the interim government. Agence France Press reports a UN representative in the conference states: "Afghan women have been silenced more than any other group, and the United Nations believes it is important to give them a chance to express their views about what they want the future of Afghanistan to be."[331]

From the London Conference on Afghanistan in 2006, emerged the "Afghanistan Compact", through its implementation the international community wanted to build lasting Afghan capacity and effective state and civil society institutions, with particular emphasis on building up human capacities of men and women alike; recognize in all policies and programmes that men and women have equal rights and responsibilities. Target was set that by end-2010: the National Action Plan for Women in Afghanistan will be fully implemented; and, in line with Afghanistan's United Nations Millennium Development Goals, female participation in all Afghan governance institutions, including elected and appointed bodies and the civil service, will be strengthened.[332]

One of the goals of London Conference was to increase the enrolment of women in universities from the current 10,000 to 40,000. The Ministry of Education also decided to make more girls' schools and high schools. In March 2005, the UNICEF and the Ministry of Education began a national campaign to boost girls' education. It has been decided that 75,000 religious workers will be recruited in the campaign to inform the people that educating sons and daughters alike was a duty laid down by Islam.[333]

On January 12, 2002, Afghanistan signed the Declaration of the Essential Rights of the Afghan Women in Dushanbe, Tajikistan, which had been prepared by 300 Afghan women under the auspices of the NEGAR-Support of Women of Afghanistan, a French NGO. The document calls for 'equality between men and women, equal protection under the law, institutional education in all disciplines, freedom of movement, freedom of speech and political participation, and the right to wear or no to wear the burqa or the scarf.'[334] In 2003, Afghanistan signed and ratified the Convention on the Elimination of All Forms of Discrimination Against Women (CEDAW).

The Afghanistan government entered into numerous treaties and ratified various conventions internationally which pertain to women's human rights. Afghanistan became a member of:

- International Covenant on Economic, Social and Cultural Rights
- International Covenant on Civil and Political Rights
- Convention on the Elimination of all forms of Discrimination Against Women
- Universal Declaration of Human Right

It is evident from the above mentioned details that the government in Afghanistan had an obligation, (may be as a result of international pressure) to protect the women of the country. This commitment was reiterated clearly in the Afghan Constitution which was revised and brought into effect by the interim government under Karzai. The Afghan Constitution mentions the government's duty to observe and respect the rights of women:

Article 7 of the Constitution states, "The State must abide by the United Nations Charter, international treaties and international conventions that Afghanistan has signed, and the Universal Declaration of Human Rights."[335]Article 22 of the Constitution further elaborates: "Any kind of discrimination and privilege between the citizens of Afghanistan is prohibited. The citizens of Afghanistan, whether men or women, have equal rights and equal duties before the law."[336]

According to articles 43 and 44 of the Constitution the government was tasked to take necessary measures to eliminate illiteracy and develop women's education. Article 52 laid down that the state must provide free health care and medical assistance to women.[337]

In March 2005, the Afghan Supreme Court approved a new marriage contract (nikah nama) in order to check forced marriages and child marriages, and to empower women's legal status after marriage. This new marriage document stipulates that if a man wants to marry, he must first make sure that the prospective wife is at least sixteen years of age. Officially it became a legal prerequisite. Rule was passed that no marriage certificates can be issued for underage brides. This step has been appreciated and termed as 'courageous reform' by international observers.[338]

According to the Afghan National Development Strategy of 2007 that the government laid out, it had committed itself to eliminate poverty among women by at least 20%, and ensure that women make up 20% of all public bodies by the year 2010.[339] The Ministry of Women's Affairs has declared the year 2020 as the 'target year' to eliminate gender discrimination in the society at all levels.

The Convention on the Elimination of all forms of Discrimination against Women (CEDAW) that Afghanistan is signatory to, states in its article 10 that the government is obligated to make efforts to provide for equal rights of men and women in terms of education. The article 12 of the Convention goes on to say that signatory states must take necessary steps for the complete eradication of discrimination in all its forms and manifestations against women. It asked to prepare grounds for women's access to health services as well as suitable food during their pregnancy. The article 14 makes it clear that all citizens of a state will be equal before courts and tribunals, and that everyone will have the same rights to a fair public hearing by an independent and impartial tribunal in accordance with the law. According to article 16 of the same compact: "States shall take all appropriate measures to eliminate discrimination against all matters related to marriage and family relations, and in particular, shall ensure, on the basis of the equality of men and women, the same right to freely choose a spouse." According to the International Covenant on Civil and Political Rights that Afghanistan has ratified, no marriage can be entered into without the free and full consent of the intending spouses (article 23, part 3).[340]

The Judicial Reform Commission (JRC) was established in November 2002 as mandated in the Bonn Agreement, to rebuild the domestic legal *system* "in accordance with Islamic principles, international standards, the rule of law and Afghan legal traditions".[341] The JRC is responsible for preparing drafts of new Criminal, Criminal Procedure and Family Codes, and for surveying the existing judicial system in Afghanistan. It has also been involved in the training for judges.[342]

Other than that, the Afghan government, recognizing the important role that religious leaders and tribal elders can play in bringing about a positive improvement in the lives of Afghan women, has tried and continues to use religious experts to change attitudes and legitimize rights that the government is under obligation to grant to the women. *Fatwas* (religious rulings) have been issued in favour of girls' education, as well as for the political participation of women through voting in elections and being part of the democratic process. [343]

It is important to note that Afghanistan's international commitments with regard to improving the status of women at home entailed an important responsibility and was a legal obligation on the part of the interim government. According to Amnesty International, "the international standards provide the essential framework for developing national legislation and measures to uphold women's human rights. The government of Afghanistan has the responsibility under international human rights law, and must take every possible step to ensure that women's human rights are protected throughout all stages of the reconstruction process."[344] Despite obstacles some real progresses have been achieved in providing economic opportunity to women. Two significant vehicles for that were

National Solidarity Programme and microcredit support for small scale enterprise. An article in Foreign Affairs described it as "the most widely held development programme in Afghanistan."[345] Undoubtedly, these were momentous developments, especially compared with the previous regime yet the condition of women in contemporary Afghanistan remains complex.

These achievements are real and should not be underestimated. Yet huge challenges remain and too many women are still denied rights that should be taken for granted. Even now, a woman who runs away from home to escape domestic abuse is seen as dishonouring her family and often loses the right to see her children. Debates over the degree to which cultural mores should penetrate state law and policy more often than not revolve around the issue of women's rights. The sad irony is that in Afghanistan the crusade for women's rights has become symbolic for both sides of the conflict, weakening the situation of all women caught between.[346] The process leading up to the adoption of the Constitution establishes that a space for women civil society activists have emerged emerge in Afghanistan. Many Civil Society Organizations (CSO), Non-Governmental Organization (NGO) and International NGOS (INGOS)have encouraged and insisted that gathering of women together is very important. They have received funding for bringing together women on a variety of pretexts. These organizations have attempted to empower women of the country through various types of training, business opportunities, exposure etc.

While the government and the international partners of the new regime have made considerable effort in this regard, a true assessment of the sincerity, efficiency and success of these efforts and measures can only be made by looking at the current state of affairs with regard to Afghan women. The next section focuses on the 'other side' of the picture, the effects and results of the new policies and efforts, and the lives of women in Afghanistan today.

The "Other Side" of International intervention for Afghan Women

The Interim Afghanistan National Development Strategy (ANDS), approved at the London Conference along with the Afghanistan Compact, contained a total of 18 statements of commitment addressing gender equity.[347] The ANDS noted that "[a]n important precondition for the success of Afghanistan's development goals is the reversal of women's historical disadvantage in Afghan society."[348] The ANDS also included a Gender Equity Cross Cutting Strategy (AGE-CCS), an overarching framework "to ensure that the overall outcomes of ANDS will significantly improve the status of women and avoid inadvertent negative impacts on their lives."[349] The AGE-CCS was "a means through which the government, in partnership with the international community, NGOs, and other sectors of society, was expected to continue to fulfill its commitments to women as provided in national policies and international treaties."[350] The National Action Plan for the Women of Afghanistan (NAPWA) was a 10-year plan of action by the Government of Afghanistan to implement its commitments to women constituents, focusing on six sectors: security; legal protection and human rights; leadership and political participation; economy, work and poverty; health; and education. It included a comprehensive analysis of women's circumstances in each of the mentioned sectors, a product of a two-year consultation between the UN Development Fund for Women (UNIFEM) and Afghanistan's Ministry of Women's Affairs.[351] It identified policies and actions that needed to be implemented to address women's difficulties, taking into consideration the government's commitments under the Afghanistan Millennium Development Goals, the Afghanistan Compact and the ANDS. The NAPWA has been endorsed by 17 ministries and accepted by the President and the Social Committee of the Cabinet and UNIFEM expects it to be formally launched in the near future.[352]

However in terms of political participation, an overwhelming majority of women in Afghanistan have only limited direct contact with political institutions. The Afghan Government committed to fast tracking the increase of women's participation in the civil service at all levels to 30% by 2013. Currently, only 22% of all regular government employees are women, and only 9% percent of these are at the decision-making level.[353] In the 9,394 Community Development Councils established throughout Afghanistan by May 2007, the number of female members was 21,239 (24%), compared to 67,212 (76%) male members. While women represent 27% of the National Assembly, the Minister of Women's Affairs was the only female cabinet member, and in 17 of 36 ministries there are fewer than 10% female employees.[354] There was an Afghan Women Judges Association, created in 2003, and an Afghan Women Lawyers and Professionals Association. The Family and Juvenile Courts are headed by women, but of the 1,547 sitting judges in Afghanistan only 62, or 4.2%, are female. Of the 546 prosecutors, 35 (6.4%) are female, and of the 1,241 attorneys 76 (6.1%) are female. There are no women members in the Supreme Court Council.[355]

Throughout Afghanistan, "it is a cherished ideal that the men of the household should be the breadwinners, while women take care of domestic chores. However, most households cannot live up to this ideal, and women contribute in a variety of ways to the family's upkeep."[356] As discussed in the previous chapters, in the economy of rural Afghanistan, male and female roles differ. For the most part, women and girls engage in a number of farm-based activities "ranging from seed bed preparation, weeding, horticulture, and fruit cultivation to a series of post-harvest crop processing activities such as cleaning and drying vegetables, fruits and nuts for domestic use and for marketing."[357] Therefore in rural areas, the definition of "economic activity" frequently "excludes the exchange of labor and products between households" and "post-harvest processing of crops (drying/cleaning/preserving), which is a predominately female domain." It also often exclude "the vital role women in the Southern Afghanistan play regarding a household's contracting of poppy harvesters, for whom three solid daily meals are part of their wage packet."[358]

In urban areas, women's access to the labor market "is constrained by historical circumstances, low skills, limited opportunities, stringent cultural norms, occupational sex segregation and a number of demographic factors."[359] Outside the domestic sphere, women's employment has always been subject to severe restrictions, and the limited access to childcare continues to pose a significant obstacle to women's employment outside the home. The World Bank reports that women's roles in livestock production and dairy processing are increasing, although most of their labour remains non-monetized.[360] Lack of mobility is one of the most important factors in Afghanistan women's inability to attain more economic power. Rural Afghan women who produce products for sale cannot sell these products themselves, because social mores, if not national legislation, preclude them from travelling to the bazaars. In some cases, urban women, who have been trained by NGOs in various areas for economic regeneration, cannot access jobs and opportunities due to geographical distance. For example, Indian NGO Self Employed Women's Association (SEWA) has been training Afghan women in various capacity building projects as a part of India Government's developmental initiatives for Afghanistan. Several women have been trained in various livelihood generation skills but surprisingly many of them remain unemployed even today. Abida, one of the master trainers at the Vocational Training Centre run by SEWA at *Bagh-e-Zanana* explained "it is our custom, which prohibits women to travel away from home in search of jobs. People don't mind dying out of hunger but do not want women to go away from home to take up job."[361]

Property ownership is another area where laws may not discriminate against women, but practice and tradition prevent women from taking full advantage of their rights. Afghan secular law and Shari'a law both allow for female property inheritance and ownership. However, the reality is that few women in Afghanistan inherit or own property. The situation varies by ethnic group and region, however, with Tajik women more likely to inherit land than their Uzbek or Pashtun compatriots. Educated women, particularly those with English-language skills, came of out their house for employment in the changed environment after 2005 belonged mostly to Tajik and Hazara ethnicity. Although many of the jobs they could find, such as teaching and nursing, were quite poorly paid, they did provide options.[362] Moreover, discrimination remained a factor. Cultural acceptance was one aspect of this, but legal and governmental restrictions remained at all levels and in all sectors. Female professionals in Afghanistan are rare outside of Kabul. With the exception of those responsible for juvenile and family courts, women judges were generally employed functionally as clerks, not as adjudicators.[363] If would be fallacious to assume that the changes in Afghan women's condition over the past decade has been insignificant. The progress that has been achieved has a result of rigorous effort. At the same time, it must be remembered that interpreting women's progress based on their rights and privileges provided on paper by international community, might give an incorrect picture.

Gender, Rule of Law and National Policies: Progress Made Only on Paper?

The Afghanistan National Human Development Report (2004) claimed, "Poverty dis-empowers Afghan women much more insidiously than official discrimination does. As long as women are focused on meeting their own and their families' basic needs for food, water, and shelter, they are effectively blocked from seeking real power via education, activism, and legislation."[364] After the fall of Taliban the women expected much from the reconstruction. However by 2007, much of the optimism about Afghanistan entering a new area of peace, security and development that prevailed in the initial years after intervention had been swept away.

The overwhelming majority of women even today have only limited direct contact with political institutions. The Afghan Government recently committed to fast tracking the increase of women's participation in the civil service at all levels to 30% by 2013. Even after years of intervention, the investments that could have increased demand for female labour has not been made and women's unemployment in urban areas continue to be abysmally high. Limited levels of skill and low demand for female labour lock women into restricted range of income generation activities. In Kabul and a few other urban centres, a small number of women work for international NGOs, UN Organizations, foreign embassies and ISAF. These are the women who have good command over English language and in most cases they have been brought up on exile societies in English speaking countries or have had access to very good quality of education in others countries were they migrated. This section obviously represents only a microscopic minority of the women population. Attempts to address the problems of majority of women in Afghanistan have been grossly inadequate. Rural poverty, landlessness and homelessness have resulted in the mass rural to urban labour migration. Despite continuing social restriction on women a large number of internal migrants were women, but conditions of work for women in urban areas were more exploitative than men. This economic servitude -just as much as the customary practices continues to keep Afghan women in their place. The 'place' is always in some man's home, under some man's control. When asked to a working girl from Kabul (who expressed her unwillingness to get married ever!) about the compulsion of an economically independent Afghan girl to be controlled by a man she expressed:

> "People would think they are prostitutes...forget about single independent women, even a widow must live with her keen, be it father or brother. If a woman likes her family or if her husband treats her well, she is lucky. But her real socio-economic status is that of a 'slave'".[365]

Women's rights groups both national and international claim that women in Afghanistan at present have a variety of rights they did not enjoy earlier. In practice, however, one finds that the changes inducted by the topmost forces of the administration have not quite filtered through to the grassroots as of yet.[366] A Ministry for 'Women's Affairs' was something previously unknown in Afghan governance, this was established under the watchful eyes of international community after Bonn 2001. It held the promise of great change for Afghan women, though the first minister, Sima Samar, who had spent much of her life working for women's rights was apparently discouraged from doing "too much" by her male colleagues even before the plane carrying the new cabinet touched down in Kabul and Samar was soon erased out of office without ever being assigned a telephone.[367] The women at MOWA even today talks about their limited capacity since the department doesnot have any budget allocation, "Even if we want to do something, we are unable to do, our hands are tied."[368] MOWA did manage to hangout a banner saying: GREAT LEADERS HAVE GREAT MOTHERS, while the department did not have their own funds to purchase even a heater or telephone. By 2012, the ministry had become a "Kabuli Joke", said a women who has been dealing with the department for 5 years for her NGO.[369]

Whatever little impact that could have been brought through works of NGOs, Civil Society Organizations and MOWA could not be achieved because of the atmosphere of insecurity. The government is as yet unable to restore an atmosphere of security and stability. In fact, human rights activists complain of being subjected to intimidation and threat. The former head of the Ministry of Women's Affairs Safia Amajan was shot dead, and security threats keep numerous others indoors. A worker at the MOWA Headquarters says, "Women in Afghanistan today no more want to step out of their homes due to the atmosphere of insecurity."[370] Though women in Afghanistan have managed to hold 25% of seats in the parliament, female politicians and activists face intimidation and violence. Brita Fernandes Schmidt of Womankind Worldwide says, "My message to the international community is that you need to address specific security issues for women. Activists are being killed and it is not going to be changed unless drastic action is taken."[371] Independent organizations and activists working in Afghanistan criticize the government for failing to provide security and materializing commitments made, by not seeing them through to implementation.

The gaping loophole is that the current political setup has accommodated numerous elements of the anti-Taliban and pro-US/NATO Northern Alliance with a criminal past record. Warlords of yore rule the roost and enjoy power which is used to maintain the status quo for women. Besides, the unlimited powers these warlords enjoy at the behest of their foreign backers give them a free hand in managing international funds and aid, most of which is embezzled and is hence not spent on development and humanitarian assistance work. Corruption has been a major impediment in the task of raising the status of women in Afghanistan. Mariam Rawi of the Revolutionary Association of the Women of Afghanistan believes the government has fallen into the hands of criminals and looting and destruction is being carried out without check. The Northern Alliance warlords who spread chaos from 1992-1996 before the Taliban takeover left behind a legacy of tens of thousands of deaths and destruction as well as homelessness. They are ruling again with guns and money and the real power behind them, the United States of America, is letting it be. She said:

> "You might expect me to talk about Afghanistan as a free, peaceful and liberated country, but painfully and unfortunately the reality is not what you might be aware

> of through the media. After 9/11, subsequent military intervention in Afghanistan in the name of the War on Terror and liberating Afghan women_ despite the tall claims of the United States and its allies_ Afghanistan is still burning in a two-fold fire. On one hand the Northern Alliance warlords supported by the US and on the other hand the Taliban and Al Qaeda terrorists supported by clandestine groups internationally; and moreover, an administration, legislature and judiciary under the domination of criminals and traitors will never do any good for our bereaved people. Treacherousness and corruption has meshed around the roots of the government very deeply."[372]

The Revolutionary Association of the Women of Afghanistan (RAWA) also reports that of the $10 to 12 billion received in aid from its international donors, not even a billion has been spent on the people of Afghanistan.[373] Dr. Ramzan Bashar Dost, Afghan Member of Parliament says, "Even if just one billion of aid money had been spent honestly, Afghanistan would have changed."[374] The Washington Post acknowledged that there exist 'serious flaws in American efforts to rebuild Afghanistan.'[375] Corruption and inefficiency are rife and millions of dollars have been wasted on 'useless projects.' In a still more scathing critique in its 2007 *Communique*, the RAWA reports that :

> "after seven years there is no peace in Afghanistan. Destitution and suffering has doubled. Our people, especially women and children fall victim to fighting, non-stop US-NATO bombardments and terror attacks. The Northern Alliance bloodsuckers (sic) who are part of Karzai's team with key government posts continue to be the most serious obstacle

> towards the establishment of peace and democracy in Afghanistan. Human rights violations, crime and corruption have reached their peak, so much so that the president is now forced to request his MPs to 'keep some limits."[376]

In its report on human rights situation in Afghanistan pertaining to women, the Human Rights Watch maintained that women in the country today are still extremely vulnerable to reprisal at the behest of the different factions in the ongoing infighting. The prevalent insecurity restricts severely the activity and opportunities for women. The worst hit among Afghanistan's suffering woman kind were the women in the refugee camps who live in miserable conditions, as well as the numerous war widows struggling to survive. Kabul alone has around 40-50,000 war widows in dire need of rehabilitation. [377]Extreme poverty, lack of means of earning or a male relative to depend on along with children and dependents to support compels these despondent women to take to begging, petty crime or prostitution. As a result, the number of criminal women is increasing and this naturally has a disastrous effect on families. This devastation is the consequence of the decades of war and oppression in the country. Besides, interviews conducted by the Human Rights Watch with refugees along the Pakistan-Afghanistan border reveal that women in the refugee camps are invariably victims of widespread abuse.[378]

Violence Against Women

Majority of Afghan women experience violence in every aspects of their lives, both in public and private, in the community and the family. Violence against women in the family including physical abuse and underage marriage is widely reported. Forced and underage marriage also occurs when women and girls are given in marriage as a means of dispute resolution by informal justice mechanisms. Rape of women and girls by armed groups continues to occur. The prevalence of violence against women and girls constitutes a grave threat to their right to physical and mental integrity. Abuse and violence suffered by Afghan women takes various forms. Some of them have been discussed below:

Domestic (Family) Violence

Violence against women in the home by husbands, male family members and, on rarer occasions, female family members is widely reported. Majority of women in both rural and urban areas are faced with family violence. The Afghan Independent Human Rights Commission's report shows 50% of women undergo daily beatings at home. Few cases of abuse, however, are reported either to the authorities or NGOs. Severely injured women seek treatment at hospitals all over the country. According to one woman doctor interviewed by Amnesty International, "domestic and physical violence are normal practice – we have a lot of cases of broken arms, broken legs and other injuries. It is common practice in Afghanistan – it is not something we should say is not in our region because most Afghan men are using violence."[379] A foreign doctor working in a hospital spoke of women victims of severe domestic violence undergoing hospital treatment at a rate of about one each week. No monitoring of domestic violence issues is undertaken and the doctor stated that she believed domestic violence often went unrecognized.

The BBC reported a young mother of three who suffered systematic daily violence at home. She narrated, "My man beats me whenever he feels like. He broke my arms, then legs, and now again he has broken my arm. I try not to make a fuss about it for the sake of my children."[380] Such women, according to the local police, keep turning up in ever-increasing numbers. The police themselves feel helpless against this.[381] Another beaten woman expressed, "The police have been to see my husband several times, and they made him sign a written undertaking not to beat me any more. But it just does not make any difference. I've asked my brother and my parents to help, but they say we are a very poor family and cannot afford to take you back."[382]

Subjection to continual physical violence is extremely traumatizing and results in chronic depression which at times is so severe that it can drive the victim to suicide and violent death through self-immolation. Suicide and self-immolation rates in Afghanistan remain high and the single most important reason for this is domestic violence and abuse which goes on unabated. It lead to drug abuse by women seeking escape, rising prostitution and escape from home due to violence and severe restrictions. [383]AIHRC reported that in Kandahar alone, there were over 300 women seeking shelter at rehabilitation centres who have escaped domestic violence at home. Tragically, however, on discovery of having 'run away' by the family, the victimizers get the woman back and subject her to even more violent punishment than she had sought escape from.[384]

Underage Marriages

The legal age for marriage in Afghanistan for men has been set to be 18 and for women 16 years. . In Afghan civil law, the legal age of marriage is given in the article 71 of the Constitution, which states that "Marriage or the consummation of marriage is not allowed before the age of 16."[385] However, in reality it is quite rare to find a girl, particularly in rural areas, who are unmarried at 16. Amnesty International asked focus groups of women about the typical age of marriage in their communities. All groups gave the age at which girls married as typically between 12 to 16 years. A women's *shura* (traditional Afghan decision making body) in Nangarhar Province in eastern Afghanistan reported marriage age for girls to be between 10 and 12 years in the region. On occasion, girls are forced into marriage below the age of puberty, sometimes at extremely young ages.[386]Such cases include that of Fariba, aged eight, who was given in marriage to a 48-year-old man. The father of the girl reportedly received 600,000 Afghani for his daughter. Fariba was reported to have suffered sexual abuse by the husband. There exist countless such stories, and few girls have the opportunity to express their distress.[387]

Humaira Daqiq, a policewoman in Kabul is reported by the BBC saying "Due to poverty many parents marry their daughters off to wealthy old men when the girls are still very young and often when they are underage."[388] Humaira, an 18 year old student at Mazar e Sharif was promised in marriage to a much older man when she was just a few months old. He later returned to claim her and she was distraught. "I went to the police but they could not help me. His family says if I do not go through with the marriage then my father should kill me." [389]The trend of underage marriages has dampened down the chances of women acquiring education or pursuing careers.

Forced Marriages

Forced marriages are those that do not have the consent of the intending spouses, and are contracted under pressure or through the use of force by a third party within or without the family. According to law and international conventions Afghanistan is signatory to, clear and explicit consent by both partners is required before a marriage can be contracted. However, the law has been routinely violated in Afghanistan and in most cases never punished by authorities. The roots of this practice again reach deep into the traditions of Afghan society. Women in focus groups in a survey conducted by Amnesty International described marriage practices that denied them the right to choose a spouse. A husband would be chosen by the father or another close male relative, and the marriage imposed upon girls and women, if necessary in the face of protest and against their will. This oppressive process reflects in part the fact that girls and women have been treated as an economic asset, with families receiving a price from the family of the groom on marriage in all communities where Amnesty International conducted research. They are also reflective of the pervasive control exerted by husbands and male relatives on women's lives. [390]

The prime reason for forced marriages is the use of women to settle family or tribal feuds. In such cases huge dowries are generally demanded and women are subjected to entering into engagement without their consent. In Afghanistan today, 50% of women get married not merely without their consent, but positively against their will and are hence not happy with their spouses, leading to disturbed family life and worse still, domestic violence.[391] MOWA stated that at present two in every five marriages that take place in Afghanistan are forced. [392]Another survey conducted by Womankind Worldwide shows that 60-80% of marriages in Afghanistan are forced. [393]According to a survey conducted by the United Nations News Centre, most people in Afghanistan believe the primary reason for violence against women was forced and child marriages. Forced marriages can lead to drastic consequences, and often the husbands who are generally much older to their young wives, subject them to sexual abuse and violence. An even more heinous practice is marrying daughters by force to families who later use them as prostitutes to bring income for the family. The law seems to be helpless against this as 'in only a very small fraction of cases will any sanction be imposed on perpetrators of domestic violence.'[394]

Exchange Marriages or Trading of Women

In Afghanistan, marriages take place with intimidation by powerful people in order to repay debts. Poor families who cannot afford to pay off debts in cash, sell off their daughters as chattel under pressure from creditors. Other than that, families also resolve disputes with other families or tribes by handing over daughters in marriage, or exchanging girls through marriage. Blood feuds are settled through the same practice. Women are exchanged instead of blood money to avenge murders. Naturally, the woman is later subjected to extreme violence, abuse and punishment as the second family 'sees the killer in her.' Forced marriage of girls and women also occurs as a result of decisions of *jirgas*. People report the giving of girls, usually below the legal age of marriage, as the preferred means of resolving cases of unintentional killing. Typically, the family of the perpetrator will be ordered to provide a girl, or girls, to the family of the deceased, in order to compensate for the alleged crime. Girls "exchanged" are then forcibly married to male members of the victim's family.

Girls exchanged in marriage or given as chattel are treated very badly after marriage.[395] Amnesty International reported, "Women speak of the particularly harsh treatment of girls given in dispute resolution and subsequently married. Their own families might sever contact with them, and the family of the groom regards them as tainted by the circumstances of the marriage."[396]

Girls in Afghanistan have been used as currency and this trend has intensified due to poverty and infighting in which blood feuds and disputes are settled through this practice. Many Afghan poor families sell their daughters as brides. Nazir Ahmad who lived in Jalalabad was forced to pay a debt of less than $200 by selling his 16 years old daughter to marry the lender's son. RAWA investigated about 500 cases of girls given in marriage to settle blood feuds and found only four or five that ended happily. Such girls are often beaten and sometimes killed because when the family looks at her, they see the killer.[397]

Sexual Abuse and Rape

Girls and women married by force below the legal age or those who were used as chattel happened to be the worst victims of sexual abuse by the male members of the family. Other than that, sexual harassment of women, sexual sadism and marital rape have also been common all over the country. Due to the notion of 'honour' involved, such cases are almost never reported. Amnesty International reports, "The exact extent and prevalence of such abuses remains unclear owing to the reluctance of most victims to speak out and the limited capacity for monitoring."[398]

Abuses perpetrated by armed groups and military forces against women and girls since the fall of the Taleban government in November 2001 include rape, abduction, and forced and underage marriage. The failure to establish security and legitimate government in many parts of Afghanistan has left women and girls at continuing risk of rape, sexual violence and intimidation. They are extremely vulnerable today to rampant sexual abuse and assault by the different factions in the ongoing infighting, in the face of which the interim government seems to be utterly powerless to exert control.

In its October 2008 official statement, the Revolutionary Association of the Women of Afghanistan (RAWA) states: "The country has been turned into a mafia state and rape and abduction of women and children has no parallel in the history of Afghanistan. Rapists are not only protected from prosecution due to their influence, but have even been forgiven as Karzai announced a general amnesty."[399] RAWA reported that eleven year old Rahima, 14 year old Fatima and her mother were raped by are lords and gunmen. In another case 9 year old Saima was tortured and raped by warlords as punishment for her father's crime. Human rights are in crises as criminal warlords hold high office and child abuse and gang rapes are on the increase.[400]

Amnesty International's research indicates a systematic pattern of abuse against women and girls in Mazar-e Sharif, and incidents of abuse in both Nangarhar and Bamiyan provinces. Human Rights Watch has reported on the occurrence of rape of women, girls and boys in southeast Afghanistan, including in Laghman, Ghazni, Gardez and Nangarhar provinces, and in Paghman district of Kabul province. Incidents reported to Amnesty International included the rape of four girls by members of an armed group. The youngest, aged 12, was unconscious as a result of her injuries when brought to hospital by her parents. UNAMA has investigated a number of incidents of abuse of women and girls by members of armed groups, including incidence of forced marriage of girls as young as 12.[401]

In its report on human rights violation in Afghanistan Amnesty International stated:

> "Amnesty International is deeply concerned by reports that in certain cases, members of the police or the Afghan National Army (ANA) may be involved or colluding in such abuses.

> In one incident, said to be indicative of a pattern of abuse, a woman was reported to have been detained at an ANA checkpoint and handed over to the commander of an armed group. Her fate remained unknown, but it was understood that she would be transferred as a "gift" to different commanders. Amnesty International was informed of incidents of police colluding in such abuses. There are also reports of women's reluctance to report such abuse because they fear government involvement. One individual told Amnesty International, "These cases remain secret because if a government official becomes aware they will start abusing the woman".[402]

Due to the weakness of the criminal justice system, and the fact that it was dominated by the influence of misogynistic and criminal elements, seeking justice for victimized women was almost impossible.[403] Women reporting rape run the risk of being imprisoned for having committed adultery outside marriage, especially if the rapist happens to be a person of influence.[404] There also is evidence that cases relating to women have been judged unfairly. Investigation of crimes against women is poorly carried out both due to lack of will and lack of resources. Warlords continue to intimidate women's rights activists. Courts pay little attention to such issues and decisions are often made in the absence of the woman involved, because the family's sense of honour does not allow the woman to be presented in public.[405] There is increased vulnerability of women to abuse owing to the involvement in some cases of commanders or members of armed factions in the criminal justice system.

An increasing incidents of sexual abuse have been reported among women in prisons. No safeguards are in place to protect women from sexual abuse while in police custody. Amnesty

International has received reports of sexual abuse of women prisoners in official detention centres in Herat, Mazar-e Sharif and Kabul. In Herat in early 2003, a riot by women prisoners were alleged to have been a response to sexual abuse by staff. Assaults by staff and incidents of members of armed factions being allowed to abuse women prisoners were reported in Mazar-e Sharif. When women were arrested for adultery, they again faced the risk of sexual abuse and transfer to different police stations where they were repeatedly abused. One woman told Amnesty International: "If the commanders arrest a girl in a case of adultery when her case is going to the first district police station, they are sexually abusing her saying you had relations with a man so you should with us also. Then they transfer the woman from station to station."[406]

Honour Killings

Ms. Hannah Irfan, a Human Rights lawyer defines 'honour killing' as an act of murder of a person assumed or alleged to be guilty of what is seen as sexual transgression by the victim's family tarnishing the family's sense of honour.[407] The 'sense of honour', the violation of which leads to violence on the victim leading to death, has been a part of Afghan tribal tradition. The incidence of honour killings in the country has been on the rise and often involves influential families. Women are judged to have committed sexual transgression through primitive tribal jirgas, which decree punishment on the woman by the family which considers itself to have been shamed by the act. The punishment almost invariably, is death. No due legal process is required in such cases.

Due to this strong notion of 'honour', no woman is to be seen in public unaccompanied by a man. Women seen 'unaccompanied' are usually suspected of sexual offences. Moreover, women who seek escape from domestic violence or forced marriage are also alleged with illicit sexual activity. The United Nations News Centre reported, "Once a woman has spent even a single night away from family control, it becomes a dead end in her life. The stigma attached with this makes her be refused by her family, or accepted only to face punishment, often death."[408]

Amnesty International received reports of women and girls killed by family members. These included the shooting of a woman by her father for refusing his choice of husband. The district governor of the woman's village attempted to bring the alleged killer to justice, but was frustrated in his efforts when the alleged killer was given sanctuary by members of an armed group to whom he is reportedly affiliated. Amnesty International also received reports of two 12-year-old girls killed by their husbands. Amnesty International's research indicated that in some parts of the country custom or tradition is used to legitimize the violent deaths of women. In eastern Afghanistan, wherever women and girls are alleged to have committed adultery or eloped, the family deals with the situation by killing the woman involved. In some parts of Afghanistan, adultery, "running away from home" and unlawful sexual activity are invariably, and with or without circumstantial evidence and due legal procedure, punishable by death. Some women in such circumstances are also at risk of being killed if released.[409]

According to Yakin Erturk, the Special Rapporteur of the United Nations Human Rights Violations against Women, forced and child marriages, physical and sexual abuse and honour killings on the orders of local warlords along with rising self-immolation cases have become a 'dramatic problem' in Afghanistan. He further states, "The violence has to come to an end. There is no reason under the sun that can legitimize any of these acts, and if the government is going to gain legitimacy and credibility, it has to find ways of dealing with these issues... Girls burn themselves to death because they have no other way to escape violence, not only from husbands, fathers and fathers-in-law, but even mothers-in-law."[410]

The international NGO Womankind Worldwide reported in 2008, "Seven years after the US invasion, gender violence has reached shocking and worrying levels in Afghanistan and efforts must be redoubled to tackle it. Our findings clearly indicate that that despite over 6 years of international rhetoric about Afghan women's emancipation and development, a real tangible change has not touched the lives of millions of women in the country. Guarantees given to Afghan women after the Taliban have not translated into real change."[411] In its official *Communique* in 2008, the Revolutionary Association of the Women of Afghanistan (RAWA) states: "After the United States and its allies invaded Afghanistan seven years ago, they misleadingly claimed to bring peace and democracy to liberate Afghan women from the bleeding fetters of the Taliban. However, in reality Afghan women are still burning in the inferno of violence. Women are exchanged with dogs, girls are gang-raped, men kill their wives viciously and violently...".[412]

Other than the spate of violence victimizing women, there have been also numerous other forms of injustice and discrimination that the women of Afghanistan routinely suffer, and most of these relate to the weaknesses and flaws in the legal system of Afghanistan and its feeble implementation. In its report 'Justice Denied', Amnesty International identified these problems faced by women as:[413]

- Restrictions on mobility and public life due to insecurity
- Lack of access to the right of divorce
- Lack of information and awareness of women's rights

- Inefficiency of the Criminal Justice System
- Lack of adequate provisions for women in the legal system
- Failure of police and courts to investigate crimes against women
- Failure to investigate rape and forced marriage
- Pressure by influential people on the Judiciary
- Women's inability to reach courts of law
- Confusion and lack of clarity about laws
- Lack of adequate training and capacity in state institutions
- Under-representation of women in the criminal justice system
- Inadequate provision for shelter and legal aid for women

Every year, on the first day of the month following *Ramazan* Muslim celebrate the Eid-al-Fitr. After a month of fasting and discipline, it is celebrated by pardoning prisoners in Afghanistan. Karzai government pardoned a disproportionate number of women in 2003.[414] In theory only certain people are eligible for presidential pardon-petty offenders, the old or infirm, parents leaving children unattended and prisoners who have served a huge chuck of time in most cases were among them. It is widely believed in Afghanistan, the international pressure played a huge role in Karzai's decision to pardon women along with men. Perhaps the world wanted to see a "new Afghanistan" which is nice to women. Questions have been posed as to why follow the legal procedures and why have defense consels if ultimately the prisoner will be released at Eid?

How International Community Lost the Plot in Afghanistan

Conversation between a Western journalist(WJ) and an Afghan Lawyer(AL) at a Women's Prison in Kabul.[415]

WJ: "*You see, all these women at the prison are victims of domestic violence.*"
AL: "*What is that?*"
WJ: "*In my country it is against the law for a husband to force his wife to have sex when she doesn't want to*".
AL: "*In Afghanistan not.*"
WJ: "*In my country it is against the law for husband to hit his wife.*"
AL: "*In Afghanistan not*".
WJ: "*In my country it is against the law to force a young girl to marry an old man she doesn't want to marry*".
AL : "*In Afghanistan not. In my country is custom*".

It is well known fact, when trying to lead people to an understanding on women's rights or to change mindset of people is to start from where they are. The international community through showed their commitment to address Afghanistan's in several Conferences and Conventions since 2001 and committed billions of dollars, the fact remains it failed to address issues which I required to. Several factors have been cited over the years by analysts, some blamed at the rampant corruption in Afghanistan, some to the shifting of US attention to Iraq, while others blamed to huge amount of money that was spent of hiring foreign experts who apparently were sent to provide 'solution' to Afghanistan's problems. These experts in most cases were completely divorced from the ground realities of Afghanistan often prescribed 'solutions' which turned out to be ineffective. Ann Jones book *Kabul In Winter* depicts several examples based on authors experiences in Afghanistan. She wrote how an international NGO brought an American fashion expert to trains girls in garment making. Author writes how the expert was obsessed in chasing "the market" and in the process she cut silks that the girls had saved for special order. The women whom she was brought to train wove the silk cloths after days of time and effort. The expert cut, and stitched and pressed as required untill the entire fabric was gone and so was the American fashion expert, leaving behind piles and piles of costly Mary Lou Modes, that nobody was interested to buy. In the end the expert had made money for her service while the NGO lost them.

Anna Hozyainova, Director Research of an Afghanistan based NGO, Afghanistan Public Policy Research Organization (APPRO) shared her experience of working with an UNDP expert. The project they were working together on was on public toilets in Kabul. The expert submitted his plan almost in accordance with the plan which has been working in America. His plans have been applauded in several other western societies and that is why his expertise was sought in Afghanistan. The experts plans for public toilets in Kabul also got approved by higher authority. At that point of time Ms. Hozyainova pointed at a fundamental problem in the plan. The master architect had kept men's as well as women's toilet within 2 meters that is side by side, the way it commonly exists in western societies- "and that was absolutely inappropriate" for Afghan society.[416] Having lived in Afghanistan for more that 5 years and with her experience of working with Afghan women she know that women would never be able to use a toilet where men will be around. Therefore, when the pilot project failed miserably, the expert agreed to change his plans according to the requirement of the Afghan society and its people.

It is true that there are numerous such examples which would indicate at the lack of depth and superficial approach of the international community in dealing with Afghanistan's problems, especially people's mindset which were created over centuries. Like Marriam, a young girl who works at the

British Embassy in Kabul said, "give us some time, I am sure we can do better that what we are doing now. Believe me, Afghans are trying…true, not all but some are really trying to change things for future generations". Marriam was in a party, when the discussion was taking place, she added "in the past few years this have changed in Afghanistan, may be it was not as fast as people thought it would be, may be it was not uniform but things did change. I could not imagine that I will be able to be in a gathering like this with so many men around… if this could be possible like so may other this which looked 'impossible' just a few years back, I am sure we will do better in future." [417]Marriam was not the only women who wanted to highlight at the positive developments in the past decade instead of focusing overtly on what could not be achieved, the younger generation of people in Kabul especially feels that the world should also look at the positive changes that have taken place. As Arif says while taking a bite at the burger at Afghan Fried Chicken the Afghan version of KFC, "I completely fail to understand why are foreigners obsessed with burqa clad women in Afghanistan, why cant they see that today a working girl can have lunch in a place like AFC, all alone", he said indicating at a girl who was having a bite at a table near his. Arif adds "this is a huge transformation, nobody could imagine this ever, today it is reality…who knows this can just be the beginning." [418]Young Afghans like Arif and Marriam want the world to recognize the small steps Afghan women have taken over the years, the next chapter attempts at that.

Chapter-V

WOMEN'S VOICES IN CONTEMPORARY AFGHANISTAN

Voices calling for a dignified place for women in Afghan society have been raised over many centuries. Rabi'ia Balkhi[419] (10th Century), a legendary figure Persian literature was possibly the first poetess in the history of new Persian poetry, ended her life when denied the right to marry the man of her choice. Mahasty (10th Century) went to jail for her liberal ideas.[420] Queen Gawhar Shad (15th Century) shared the political power with her husband King Shah Rukh (who ruled over major part of the empire curved out by his father Timur Lang) while dominating the cultural scene for fifty years.[421] Azo Ana and Zargoona (18th Century) were wise in high councils.[422] Zaynab, a scholar in both Pashtu and Dari, together with Aisha Durrani, a poetess illuminating her harem, defied 18th century proscriptions against education for women. Queen Soraya (19th Century) played a significant role along with her husband King Amanullah in the evolution of the country and specifically in championing women's issues. The girl's schools in Kabul, bearing their names today perhaps can be seen as a reflection of the high regard still accorded to these early 'spokeswomen' in Afghanistan.

In the West the history of centuries-long struggle for women's rights has about it the same flow and ebb, the same pattern of progress and backlash that leads to feminists to describe the recurrent historical period of their greatest achievement as waves. But in the West or even in countries like India, the struggle has been waged almost entirely by women, thousands of whom devoted their lifetimes to it. In Afghanistan, on the other hand, it was men in 19th and 20th century, including Amir Abdur Rahman, Mahmud Tarzi, King Amanullah and Prime Minister Daud Khan spoke out for the rights of women. They spoke out for the right of women to divorce, to own property, to exercise inheritance, step out of seclusion, pursue education and access medical treatment. Because of support from these men, the women of Afghanistan felt encouraged to function in public spaces so as to contribute to nation building. Yet, despite all efforts, Afghan women today sit at the bottom of gender development indices. The rights that women can claim today are few, and in many ways different from that of men, for those that exist under the law or under Islam are contingent upon the approval of father or husband.

The distinctive image of Afghan women is put together by atrociously low literacy, school attendance and life expectancy statistics, together with sky high maternal and child mortality rates. The western media bears down heavily on shocking incidents of violence within and outside the home, appealing jail conditions, suicides and paucity of access to health care services, education, employment, justice, politics and other sector of social development.[423] Nancy Hatch Dupree, after working on Afghan women for decades observed, many aid agencies have been emphasizing these negatives in order to attract funding. Not only them, even Afghans from time to time have intensified this stereotypical image by depicting rural women as chattel with no egos, no intelligence and no skills valued only for their reproductive services, which to Dupree are "grossly unfair."[424] The young generation of Afghans, especially in the cities are extremely conscious of the stereotypical images of their country and if a foreigner visits their country, many of them can be found making conscious efforts to make the visitor breakout of that image. "Afghanistan in not what you people think it to be",[425] as a young man in his twenties originally from Kunar Province, currently a professional based in Kabul puts it while pointing at several Shopping Malls that have come up in the last few years. While travelling together to different places in and around Kabul city, a young man working for one of the most popular Telecommunication Companies- Roshan, asked, "You have been travelling all around Kabul in the past few days, how many *Burqa* clad women did you notice?"[426], one of the Taxi drivers in Kabul shared a story about one of his many 'foreigner' passenger's frustration of not seeing 'adequate burqa clad women' during his visit in 2011. The point is not to generalise things based on one's limited experience in one particular part of a vast country and establish that what media tends to depict is completely false but the idea is to depict that these can very well be voices of younger generation of Afghans in the country, who wanted the world to view Afghans and Afghanistan in a different and positive light.

It is well to shine the spot light on the many inadequacies women face as the facts cannot, and should not be denied. However, by focusing only on the negatives can be disservice to those courageous individuals who have not only laboured long and hard but also made sacrifices in order to create environment in which wrongs may be redressed. A balanced picture of realities based on an understanding of culture and history of the country would have been more constructive. The following sections attempts to look into a few, among many groundbreaking initiatives and achievements by Afghans in Afghanistan over the course of past one decade.

Hope is Vital for Living: Afghan Youths Inspires the Country to Dream about a Positive Future

Violence against women in different forms have long been continuing in Afghanistan like many other countries. The consequence of the same have caused deprivation, limitation and oppression of Afghan women in various aspects, including deprivation from learning arts, artistic activities and expression of views through various art forms. It is not only the tradition, certain customs or fanaticisms which were responsible for this, inadequate attention from the government was to a major extent responsible for the inactivity of women in the mentioned spears. The government's focus for obvious reasons went to political and military tussles resulting in opening of Government run centres for cultivation of artistic skills only in two out of 34 provinces in the country, namely Kabul and Herat.

In a way, not only women but men have been deprived from needed opportunities to promote their artistic talent. And in places where the opportunity was available, the majority of families wanted their daughters to learn in places where they have separate provisions for women. For example, the Fine Art Faculty of Kabul University, with a history of more than thirty years, has only 10 to 20 female students each years while the total number of seats available were about 300.[427] In the changes environment, after years of war, when Kabul University again got a new lease of life and students started coming back for education an encouraging trend became visible. The number of female students increased to 30, which constituted almost 10 % of total students in the faculty and Centre for Contemporary Art Afghanistan (CCAA) was established in 2007.[428]

- **Centre for Contemporary Art Afghanistan (CCAA)**

Initiatives and new approaches in arts are the needs that arise together with socio-economic developments of human society. The progess made in the era of Tomorain of Herat resulted in the establishment of Kamaluddin Behzad School to encourage artistic development. Later on progressive thoughts in the light of new economic and political structures paved the way to Industrial High School, which was considered a new move in promoting visual arts in the country.[429] The inception of CCAA, in a way symbolises the third phase of artistic development in Afghanistan. With the formation of a separate centre for women, more than 160 girls came forward to be part of the same but because of resource constrains only 60 of them could be accommodated. The idea behind the centre was to address the creative needs of talented young Afghan girls and empowering their artistic, cultural identity and generating awareness towards women's rights, social justice, democracy and open society. This is undoubtedly a huge step forward in removing the serious artistic deprivation of Afghan women. CCAA tries to enable women to use tools and be familiarized with new and advanced artistic methods and styles so that they have various tools at their disposal for expressing their thoughts, imaginations and feelings. Because of its limited reach today, it intends to provide educational opportunities for women to get distance learning training in different part of Afghanistan in near future. This is treated almost like a pilot project and its overwhelming response is encouraging the authorities to start similar centres in other parts of Kabul as well as across Afghanistan.

In a remarkably short period of time the centre has conducted exhibitions on occasions such as International Women's Day, International Day of Counter-Narcotics Funded by International organizations. One of its innovative endeavours have been the paintings and poster exhibition depicting goals of Afghanistan National Development Strategy (ANDS).

These paintings and posters of different size were displayed in various parts of Kabul city as well as in provinces by ANDS.[430] This was not only an interesting step to put across messages using innovative mediums but the fact that for the first time posters painted by women were getting publicised was a great achievement. Another interesting project was sponsored by Women of the World Foundation (WWF), in which 15 painters and female learners worked together for eight months followed by exhibitions to display their creation. The centre in its short time of establishment has held workshops in the field of art history, educational films as well. With fund UN Habitat, Goethe Institute, Centre for Contemporary Art Norway and Prince Claus Fund, Nederland it publishes *Gaahnaam-e-Honar* magazine to improve the knowledge of artists, art learners interested in contemporary arts. Fareeha Ghezal, a 2nd Year, Fine Art student at Kabul University whose works titled "Hope" (Appendix...... Pic-1) have featured in the magazine says,

> "Hope is vital for Living. This I love to portray issues of hopefulness, light and wishes in my works. Presence of CCAA will bring remarkable change in the condition of art in Afghanistan and especially in women's art. I feel contemporary paintings in Afghanistan will encounter various viewpoints, it may not be understood, because understanding it needs more time span."[431]

Holding workshops and conferences by national and internationally acclaimed artists has been one of the foremost activities of CCAA. The objective of these initiatives is to upgrade the interest and practical and theoretical knowledge of artists in various aspects and also strives to strengthen the quality of independent artists. Up to 2009, workshops in areas of conceptual art, conceptual designs, conceptual architecture, contemporary art, vedio arts and illustrations have been held.[432] The films produced in the Centre tend to focus on the unpleasant impacts of war on culture and education. Some of the films that have come out from the Centre are:

Circle: The film was about old curriculum of Afghan schools and universities, how it suffered in the years of conflict and migration.

Close Door: In this film indignation to one of the main social and cultural challenges like corruption and cultural deviation grown during the long years of war were depicted.

From the World of Darkness: This film pointed at the hidden features and policies looking for women's survival in social- backwardness and dark minds of society.

Yesterday and Today: This film looked at the culture of violence in Afghanistan in the past and the situation after the international intervention.

Hope Please and Together: The film depicted the wishes and hopes of new generations of Afghans during the period of violence.

Mobile cinema was established with the aim of identifying the contemporary arts and artists in various arts and educational Centres in Kabul and also in other provinces. The main objective of showing films through mobile cinema has been to reach out to as many people possible. Screening are held through big TV Screens as well as with the help of projectors to show people what CCAA is doing and encourage new talents to join the endeavour.

- **Afghan Women premiers Short Film at Cannes International Film Festival**

Shahbanoo Sedat, became the first female director from Afghanistan to Screen a film at the prestigious Cannes

International Film Festival in France. She directed *Vice Versa One,* a short film that tackled politics and reintegration through symbolism. The 10 minute film began with a little girl carrying a backpack into which she collects "votes". Characters, including a woman and a soldier, were symbolic of some Afghans who assimilated into the post 2001 political system. In an interview given to United Nation's Publication on Afghanistan, the twenty year old director explained "A women puts the burka into the backpack ballot box. A man with the gun doesnot put in his gun. He unwraps his turban and puts that in. It shows that some people participating in politics changed their clothes but not their ideology."[433] She also expressed that words like "democracy", "Freedom of Speech" are being used in Afghanistan these days when the fact is even the educated people do not know what they mean. She finds the role of women in Afghan politics as 'largely symbolic' and is often disappointed when they allow "the man inside them to speak".[434] Sadat faced several obstacles in making and releasing the film because it was political in nature. Despite her criticism of some politicians the Iranian born Sadat expressed her thankfulness that her family has moved back in Afghanistan and she feels that more young educated women need to come forward and take part in the political like of Afghanistan as she feels only young people with honest efforts and fresh ideas are capable of taking Afghanistan forward.

- **Afghan Girls gain opportunities through Youth Groups**

AIESEC[435] Afghanistan organized a National Young Leaders Conference in Kabul in June 2011 with 250 youth delegates from Balkh, Herat, Helmand, Kandahar, Khost, Paktia and Parwan.[436] One of the issues that got attention at the Conference was the negative impact of traditional practices in the lives of young Afghan women. From Underage marriage, early pregnancies to domestic violence were discussed in the forum. This was one of its kind of experience for the participants as well as organizers, since these were issues which were never openly discussed though their ill effects were felt by people. Over the years it has been realised to stop something wrong to happen, it is very important to recognize that. Sima Safay, a 20 year old participant from Jalalabad experessed:

> "Some unfair traditional practices have been additional 'headache' for girls. Most of the time, our parents don't allow us to participate in activities like work training, sports or to appear in Television. We need to raise people's awareness on several issues in order to expect that the unfair practices will stop."[437]

It was identified that involvement of youth in public life is essential to raise awareness in several issues and for that capacity building of Afghan youths was essential. To equip young people with the knowledge and skill to solve problems, the Ministry of Culture and Young Affairs, Government of Afghanistan and the UN Children's Fund (UNICEF), created Youth Information and Communication Centres in sixteen provinces within Department of Youth Affairs.[438]In Kunar, Laghman and Nagarhar provinces, the YICC is an umbrella organization for more than a thousand young people, offering trainings and workshops on a variety of topics.[439] For girls particularly, the centre offers a public space to discuss issues and learn from one another.

"We can see more enthusiasm in girls from their increasing number in the centre"- said Malalay Panyinda, the Director of YICC, Nangarhar in a interview given to UN Newsletter. She added "Now they can discuss problems they face and issues such as marriage, relationship, education, employment and try to find solutions of the problems through discussion... this was unimaginable a few years back."[440]Girls also have access to Vocational Training. Training of young girls, women and widows have been undertaken by several organizations across Afghanistan for have been funded by International NGOS, some as a part of Bilateral Cooperation while some based of individual efforts however the objective has been common, that is to empower women economically through enhancement of their skills.

- **Capacity Building of Afghan Women through Livelihood Training**

Building capacity and empowering the local institutions in conflict ridden Afghanistan is a challenge for the world community. A participatory approach with an aim at social empowerment of women seemed to be a possibility despite the massive restriction of political environment. The degree of development intervention depended on the extent to which institutional capacity can be built. In a situation where ingredients of institutional capacity building were not in place, 'participation and empowerment' of women through development initiatives emerged as a step for building foundation of a country which ensures quality of life. Accordingly organizations working on gender issues started devising programme for building technical and business of Afghan women. Some of the organizations, that have taken active role towards the initiative are:

> Afghan Women's Mission, Revolutionary Association of Women of Afghanistan (RAWA),Afghan Women's Network, Afghanistan Women's Council, Afghanistan Women's Education Centre, Canadian Women for Women in

Afghanistan, Feminist Majority Foundation Global Fund for Women, Medica Morale, Refugee Women in Development, Womankind Worldwide, PARWAZ, NEGAR, Voice of Women, Women for Women International, MADAR, Self Employed Women's Association (SEWA), Humanitarian Assistance for Women and Children of Afghanistan, Women's Alliance for Peace and Human Rights in Afghanistan (WAPHA), Hand in Hand Afghanistan Organization (HIHAO) etc.

In the past few years, NGOs for women in Afghanistan have worked consistently for the improvement of women's lives, and have been able to achieve success to a considerable extent. So far, almost a 100,000 women have benefited from micro financing loans through international NGOs in the country.[441] Research has been conducted on various sensitive issues regarding women, and the plight of women has been brought into the limelight, and built a strong case for women's rights advocacy and reviewing of government policy and legal stance on specific women-related issues. These organizations have also sought a return of women into public life. Today several job openings for women in fields such as education, medicine, the media and journalism exist. Radio and television broadcasts in Kabul, once again has started to feature women commentators. Units have been established by these for providing emergency obstetric care and family planning services. Women have been trained as midwives to provide domestic reproductive health services. Roughly 10,000 women have received training for several skills helping them set up small scale cottage industrial units. The training has been provided by the All Afghan Women's Union as well as Women for Women International and the Self Employed Women's Association (SEWA).[442] The plight of widows in Afghanistan has always been an area of concern. Under the World Food Programme, flour is supplied to women in refugee camps, in particular to destitute war widows or independent mothers, which allows them to bake the traditional bread and sell it for small profit. NGO Madar based in Kabul has been doing significant works with widows in particular. This has helped generate nominal income for families.

Gul Makia, mother of three daughters and one son, who undertook training in food procession from Vocational Training Centre run by Indian NGO SEWA at Bagh-e-Zanana in Kabul explained how life changed for her post training.

> "Life was tough in the refugee camps. My husband couldn't get job because of his psychological problem and in the process it worsened because I could not give him medicines. After 6 years we returned with the help of money I earned as labourer...After training, nine of us formed a group and made a business plan and produced turchi and green chutney and earned a profit of Afg. 500. It was so thrilling!" Gul Jan added, "I am very happy that I got opportunity to learn. It has brought huge change in my life. I can now pay rent, electricity bill and educational expanses of my children."

- **Scholarships provided to Afghan Youths for Education and Training**

Peace, stability and prosperity in a society depend on the education level of that country. Education stimulates the expansion of shared beliefs and the development of shared values that result in cooperation rather than conflict. Only a critical mass within any population, including women and children, who are literate and able to fully participate in making decisions that shape their future, can be in a long-term the guarantor for peace and stability in that country. Therefore in the newly approved Constitution of Afghanistan (2004), education has been made compulsory for all children up to grade nine. Children start their first year of schooling at the age of seven and Constitution also states that the Government will provide education free of charges up to university level.[443] There are three levels of education: Primary (grade 1-6), Junior Secondary (Grade 7-9) and Upper Secondary (grade 10-12). [444]All diploma and degrees are referred to as grade 13 and 14. Primarily there are three different career paths for students: religious studies, academic studies or vocational training. Most students tend to decide which path they want to take up once they graduate from grade nine. The control of the education system by Islamist of fundamentalist disposition from 1992 to 2001 left a major imprint not only on the education system but also on the way of thinking of the new generation.

With the inauguration of the National Assembly in December 2005 and the formal conclusion of the Bonn Process, Government of Afghanistan (GoA) has attempted to take steps to revive the higher education sector along with primary and secondary education. With students (who were refugees in Pakistan, Iran or other neighboring countries) returning back to Afghanistan and students graduating from high schools, the demand for higher education has seen a remarkable rise in Afghanistan. For a country that was trying to rebuild itself after years of war and destruction there was an urgent need for well-educated and professionally trained human resource pull in all the sectors of economy. Afghanistan felt a critical shortage of professionals such as engineers, technicians, academic, administrators, accountants, agriculturists and business leaders, to meet the needs of reconstruction, growth and poverty reduction. Due to the devastation caused by thirty years of conflict, the needs of addressing Higher Education become a prerequisite for the foundation of a long term development process. Several countries came forward including India, Pakistan, Turkey ,Russia and Central Asian Republics to provide scholarships to Afghan youths for undertaking Higher Education and Training programmes in these countries.

In the year 2008-2009 more than 12500 students was registered for scholarships to study abroad. Over 10000 students fulfilled the criteria of application for a scholarship and more than 6000 students were introduced to the examination board. 1566 students achieved the necessary point of numbers for scholarships. 553 students were awarded scholarship to study in India. Also other 441 students were given scholarship for study in Pakistan. Other 172 students were chosen for scholarship to Kazakhstan, 119 students for studying in Russia. 66 students were introduced for scholarships in Turkey. [445] To attract more female students to take up these scholarship programme, countries like India has decided to scale up number of scholarships. The Afghan students irrespective of gender have benefitted from these initiatives and access to quality education and exposure in foreign lands have broadened the horizon's of Afghan youths immensely. One of the Afghan boys studying in India expressed "the atmosphere in Indian Universities is generally peaceful, cooperative and conducive for education...some thing we have all missed all our lives."[446] For Afghan girls, going to foreign countries for education is "One in a life time opportunity, as one girl studying at Jawaharlal Nehru University, New Delhi puts it. She shared the benefits of these opportunities are plenty, "Firstly, safety and security- not having to worry about threat of suicide bombing that have become commonplace in my country", secondly quality of education, thirdly, welcoming attitude of students and professors and most importantly the freedom and respect we enjoy here is unbelievable."[447]

According to UN Educational , Scientific and Cultural Organization (UNESCO), the education sector in Afghanistan has improved significantly for the past 10 years. Najibullah Kamran, Director of Kabul Provincial Department of Education feels "The future of Afghanistan is dependent of how effective our education system is today. A major cause of the war was ignorance and lack of education." Overall enrolment of students increased eight fold to 7.3 million in 2010, the percentage of female students rose from around zero to 38 per cent, according to UNESCO.[448]

- **Internet access connects Afghan Women with the world online**

The UN and its partners are helping train young Afghan women to break new barriers in information technology. Hundreds of young Afghan, many of them women, are getting free computer and English training as part of ICT4 Youth- a programme created by Deputy Minister of Youth Affairs (DMoya) and United Nations Development Programme (UNDP). Today young Afghan women from urban centres are increasingly going on internet- through Facebook, Twitter, TouTube and Skype- to find and stay connected with friends and family and to promote social causes. It is true that those most likely to use Facebook are young male Afghans. Nearly half of Afghans in FB are between 18 to 24 years and one third between 25 and 34 year of age. Women account for 15 percent of Afghan users according to statistical website socialbakers.com.[449] Unlike Afghan boys, Afghan girls hardly give their original photographs in their profile instead they tend to use pictures of famous Bollywood film stars, whom they like, they resemble or they can identify with. The Afghan boys also feel that girls should not give their picture as it gives a "very bad impression about her character" said an Afghan boy whose FB account has more than 500 pictures.[450] When asked to girls whether they feel that they should enjoy equal privileges to boys in this respect, some of them expressed, they are happy with what they have got now, "we could not even imagine that we'll be able to connect to the world a few years back, we are getting so much, no regrets".[451] For many Afghan women that fact that they can communicate with their families in other part of the world through Skype or are getting access to jobs through internet is a remarkable achievement it itself. They are so delighted with these opportunities that they don't want to even compare with boys. In 2010 around 300 young Afghans were trained under ICT4Youth, nearly 4o percent of them were girls.[452] Students are trained by qualified teacher for an hour everyday in basic computer software and internet skills. To prepare the students for future employment, the course also assists with resume writing and preparation for job interview and also in enhancing English Language Skills. Samira a woman in her early 20s was proud to say "I train a group of colleagues in the Ministry of Interior." These can be little but significant steps towards a better future.

- ***SKETEISTAN:* An Innovative Endeavour to overcome difference through Sport**

Sketeistan officially opened in October 2009 next to Ghazni Stadium in Kabul, is one of the few co-educational sporting NGOs in Afghanistan that work with impoverished children working in streets of Kabul. As both an athletic centre and an educational space, Sketeistan aims to provide new skills to youth so that they gain confidence in their abilities as athletes and young leaders. The students learn drawing, calligraphy, theatre, painting, story telling, Quran study, photography, design and more, however the main sport at Skateistan remains skateboarding. The aim was to build tolerance and equity, firstly by providing educational and recreational opportunities to both girls and boys. Furthermore, the idea was to bring together a cross-section of Afghans, establishing a youth community from various ethnicities, educational levels and socio-economic backgrounds. With funding from UNAMA, it organized a series of workshops for children and teens – some focussed on the anti-poverty Millennium Development Goals (MDGs)- in celebration of International Year of Youth.

For some children who attend Sketeistan's classes, this was the only opportunity to receive schooling and take part in sports. 13 year old Wahilla in her broken English and Dari said, "I came here to learn skating. My family is very happy." She has caught air while skateboarding ina head scarf and other traditional Afghan clothes on Sketeistan's ramp. Wahilla used to sell chewing gum in Kabul and once she was brought she quickly picked up the skill and currently is one of the youngest instructors at Sketeistan. She added, "I feel happier after coming here. Even after I finish class, I want to skate more in the streets at home and at school"[453]. Another students, Farhannaz said her school teacher enrolled her in Sketeistan with her parent's support. Sketeistan's creators said in an interview given to UN newletter "Afghan Youth and United Nation" that Sketeistan is a place where sport can give young people practical experience in peace building. Bringing ethnic group and socio-economic divides, sports provide a platform for young girls and boys to come together and learn from each other. "Sports is an easy entry point. It does not matter if young people are rich of poor, educated or not. They participate in exactly the same way in sport", said Oliver Percovich. They have also taking out a Magazine named *PUL* (Bridge), depicting their ideas and programmes to attract more students. Sketeistan, definitely constitutes an integral part of a new Afghanistan that upholds hope and women's voices.

- **Teen Journalist Empower Imprisoned Youth**

Zarlash Sarmast, a 15 year old Afghan girl today produces and anchors a weekly investigative segment for *Crime Scene Afghanistan,* a coproduction between Radio Television and UNAMA. Her programme today is among the most watched programmes in the country. It is dedicated to the younger audiences primarily, however it caters to their parents as well. Sarmast believes, "With this show I am helping my generation because I investigate and Bring awareness about different problems that youth face in their communities."[454] She adds, "As a young girl, I am strongly committed to my generation, I am aware of the problems young people are facing today in Afghanistan and I want to help them",[455] her programme is her way of helping them.

She has highlighted several pertinent issues and challenges through her programme. Among her most memorable cases is of a 14 year old girl who ran off with her boy friend when her family wanted to force her to marry an older man. The girl was then sent to juvenile rehabilitation centre. It was during an interview that the girl opened her heart to Zarlash and she could feel what the other girl was going through being abandoned by her parents and her community for following her heart- "that case really moved me", she said. *Crime Scene Afghanistan,* provides a much needed voice to the youth to talk to their communities, parents to authorities and also among themselves. These voices have been sending strong messages not only to youth but also to the society about their problems, concerns, worries and struggles.

Zarlash Sarmast says that the number helpless women she has been able to reach out and touch is incredible. From her experience with teenagers who are currently serving in prison for moral crimes, she feels that they are eager to get out of prison or rehabilitation centres and restart their lives. She says "being in Afghanistan is not easy because one has to deal with many cultural traditions that limit one as a member of a community. We need to develop minds and hearts of people across generations" and her programme provided the youth with a platform where they can put forward their voices which otherwise remains unheard.

- **Afghanistan's Growing Female Police Force**

Afghanistan has 130, 000 police officers but only 1, 195 of these are women. The overwhelming majority serve as regular patrol officers with few occupying managerial positions. In January 2012, seventeen police women were awarded their diplomas underlining the importance of national police of more women officer.[456] These women have faced problems of discrimination at police stations which resulted in the drop out of many. It was realised that was improving the security situation in Afghanistan, women alike men need to come forward and take important roles and that of police women were among the most crucial ones. When international community was deciding upon areas of intervention, the capacity building and recruitment of women Afghan police forces featured prominently in the plan. The UN's long term plan was to focus on upgrading skills of female police officers and on also on their accountability towards their profession. Internal affairs transparency and police misconduct were the focus areas, while an independent oversight committee that will review internal police investigations was also in the process of establishment. Attempts have been made to improve literacy level in the police force and provide transferable knowledge and skills that will allow police to better perform their duties. The new programmes undertaken were major steps towards sustainable and effective development in Afghan National Police (ANP) human resource.

The first literacy programme for Afghan police was started in 2008 with the objective to offer literacy opportunities to 600, 000 youth and adults around the country by 2013.[457] Sixty percent of the expected beneficiaries are women. Afghan government wants to increase the number of women to 5000 by 2013.[458] Nancy Hutch Dupree said "when thinking of Afghan women don't think embroidery, think cop!"[459] Several women over the years have come forward to join Afghan police. CBS News Correspondent Mandy Clark met one woman in Kabul who explained why she's risking her life to do it. Clark reported that when Maryam's husband left her to join the Taliban, he took their son with him. Left with two young daughters, the 26-year-old went on the offensive. She signed up to join the police force. Maryam told CBS News through an interpreter, "I wanted to arrest him myself."[460]

Examples of brave women police officers such as First Lieutenant Malalai Kakar has inspired many younger generations. Kakar was one of the most high profile cops in the post 2001 Afghanistan. As Lieutenant Colonel, she was the head of Kandahar's Department of crime against women. She was the first women to join Kandahar police service in the early 80s and had been instrumental in recruiting other women into the force. She has been an important role model, judging by the increasing number of women police in the country today. Kakar received numerous death threats from Taliban but that did not stop her from performing her duties, until 28th September 2008, when she was assassinated by Taliban.

Kakar has inspired many Maryam's of today and Maryam's are likely to be role models for many other women in Afghanistan. There are just two of the many stories where the women in the country are rewriting or have attempted to rewrite their stories differently.

- **Women Consulted before Peace Process ahead of International Conference in Germany**

The nation-wide "Afghan People's Dialogue on Peace" conducted in October 2011 brought hundreds of local workers, religious scholars, business owners, journalists, teachers, intellectuals, youth and members of the returnee community into small groups of discussion.[461] Conscious attempt was made to understand women's perspectives and opinions on pertinent issues such as education, health, general services etc.[462] This was a remarkable step, since the women's issues and concerns have been highlighted by men of the country all these years. This undoubtedly was a departure from what they had experienced in the past.

Dr. Sima Samar, Chirperson of the Afghan Independent Human Rights Commission (AIHRC) and former Minister of Women's Affairs were one of the members whose opinion was taken before the Bonn Conference in Germany-2012. She highlighted, that the social rights of people have dramatically improved in the past few years. Access to education, health, infrastructure and a relatively better life implied improved human rights situation in Afghanistan. The equal rights to women and men have been acknowledged in the Afghan Constitution, which again was a huge achievement. "However this does not mean that rights are not being violated. Huge number of children, particularly girls, lack access to education and a considerable size of population still lacks basic health facilities and shelter. Women in Afghanistan continues to suffer discrimination and violence",[463] therefore she urged that the international community should not undermine human rights by compromising social justice. The fact that women's voices were given importance was a positive sign and it is believed that the international support and commitment has to continue in order to bring a paradigmatic shift in Afghanistan.

- **Afghan Women in *Shuras***

One interesting development on women's front in Afghanistan has been the initiative to involve women in women's sub- *Shuras*. Initially these were reservations as they thought that the idea entailed that men and women will have to sit together in one space and they were uncomfortable thinking about the shame such as action will bring to the women's family. However, the *maulavi* then declared that a woman in trouble or distress, with the appropriate *Hejab* could come and appeal to *Shuras* for help. Though this women's *Shuras* do not necessarily indicate gender equality but at the same time it does not remove the possibility of active women's groups in tribal and federation *Shuras*.

Range of reasons were forwarded behind the opening of *Shuras* for women, ranging from a desire to involve women in community affairs to feeling coerced by interest from donor and other funding agencies.[464] Strict conditions to women's participation in *Shuras* indicate at the obstacles these women face in forming active groups at community level. Men tend to at the security concerns for women, their 'appropriate' behaviour as dictated by *Afghaniyat* and interpretation of Islam. Tendencies have been observed among the men to control women's *Shuras*. Through it would be fallacious to think that women's *Shuras* have been extremely effective in taking women's issues ahead, none the less this would remain a significant step in Afghanistan's history.

- **Business Ventures by Afghan Women**

A few years ago, it was more like half a cent that was going to female entrepreneurs who're creating jobs and helping to build companies. Everybody from Nicholas Kristof from the New York Times to Larry Summers, the former Secretary of the Treasury and White House economic guy, said 'Listen, you want to build a society, you want to fix things, you want to make changes -- invest in the women.'[465] Encouraging women in business ventures have been a recent development and Gayle Tzemach Lemmon book named "The Dressmaker of Khair Khana", has tried to depict some of their stories. People have often dismissed women entrepreneurs in Afghanistan as if they did not exist when the truth is women have been getting families through very difficult times in that country for as long as history's been written, and certainly, during the last 30 years of conflict.

Tsemach's book depicts an incredible story of a young girl named Shahla Akbari who started a shoe label of her own named "Made in Afghanistan". Her mother was an entrepreneur who was working in a furniture business, and she saw the example of her mother and was encouraged to do something on her own. There are many examples of women who have started small and have reinvested the profit in the business. Many women have received grants, but considering the amount of capital been given to Afghanistan as aid, precious little of it actually goes to small business as seed capital.

Western media has reported stories of women who have encouraged their husbands to take up small business ventures. One of them is a women named Bakht Nazira Niazi, whose encouragement motivated her husband Khan Agha Niazi to start small jewellery business. Bakht Nazira Niazi, an entrepreneur who was involved in ladies clothing and shawl business made by Afghan women encouraged him to start a jewellery line after her customers kept asking for necklaces and earrings to accompany outfits they found at her shop. Mr. Niazi said, pointing to his wife today says "If I have this jewellery business, this belongs to her efforts...She gave me many good ideas. I am using her experience in my business."[466]In March 2011, a NGO hosted an Afghan Women First matchmaking event to link female-led companies to contracting opportunities with the United Nations, NATO military forces and Afghan government ministries. Many of the women entrepreneurs have been beneficiaries of programs started since 2002 to increasing women's business skills, including the New York-based nonprofit Bpeace's Fast Runner program, Goldman Sachs's 10,000 Women, Thunderbird's Artemis program and the Institute for Economic Empowerment of Women's Peace through Business initiative.[467] The progress made in the past few years are remarkable, however there remains a constant fear about the post 2014 scenario within them.

- **Afghanistan's Woman Crime-buster on Bike**

It's unusual for a woman to be a leader in Afghanistan but Zarifa Qazizadah became the country's only female village chief through force of personality and determination to get things done - even if that means cross-dressing, wearing a false moustache and driving around on a motorbike at night. When the mother of 15 first sought political office, and told local men she wanted to connect the village to the electricity grid, they laughed. That was in 2004. She lost the election, but she got the electricity all the same, and two years later the men asked her to apply for the post of head of the village - Naw Abad in the country's northern Balkh province. Now she guards the electricity supply with a vengeance, and if anyone wires their home up and starts stealing it, they have to watch out. "I tell the men of the village, all I want is your prayers," Zarifa says. "When you have a problem, I'll speak to the government on your behalf and whenever there is any disturbance at night-time, I'll pick up my gun and come to your house to see what's going on."[468]

Women today hold quite a few powerful position in Afghanistan. Habiba Sarabi became the first female governor in Afghanistan in Bamyan province in 2005. Fawzia Koofi was the first female deputy speaker of the Afghan parliament after the women's reservation was passed in the Afghan Parliament. Qazizadah is not the first woman to have held the position of village chief - another woman in a nearby village beat her to it, but she recently died. Women in rural Afghanistan are rarely seen riding motorbikes alone and Qazizadah disguises herself, with the clothes and a fake moustache, to avoid attracting too much attention. She has also been known to come to the rescue of her villagers by wrestling Jeeps out of ditches with a tractor. To keep her promise to voters on the electricity supply, even though she failed in her bid to get elected to parliament, she travelled to the Afghan capital, Kabul, with her four-year-old daughter and went straight to the home of the Minister for Power, Shaker Kargar, demanding to speak to him. [469]He agreed to see her the following day in his office, and by the end of the meeting he had given his consent. There was one problem - the village itself had to pay for the posts and cables. Qazizadah, who had already sold some of her jewellery to pay for the trip to Kabul, borrowed money wherever she could and remortgaged her house to raise the necessary capital.

Now aged 50, with 36 grandchildren, she is head of the local women's council, as well as village head, and hosts large meetings of local women in her home, encouraging them to follow her example. "I was just a housewife like you," she told a group of 50 women at one of her recent gatherings. "But today I can have a meeting with 1,000 people. I can meet and discuss issues with authorities. If women are brave and they can achieve a lot."[470]

- **Afghan Girl makes Country Proud in London Olympics**

Tahmina Kohistani, the only Afghan female athlete at the London Olympics 2012, might have finished last in the 100 metres race but she said competing in front of 80,000 spectators made her feel like a champion. "From the beginning, I did not think about winning a gold. Being here is important. Right now I have my gold medal," she was quoted saying.[471] Kohistani, who hopes that her presence at the Games will help break barriers preventing women from practising sport in her country also said "I know getting a medal in the Olympics is very difficult, but I am here to open a new era for the women of Afghanistan,". Wearing long black trousers, long sleeves and a head scarf with the colours of green, red and black to honour the national flag, Kohistani looked quite different from the other sprinters when her pictures were published in newspapers across the world. Here's was an inspiring story, a story that again forced the world to think about the changing picture of Afghanistan. In London she expressed "In my society, there is no sport for females. My people do not accept sport for women. They think sport is not good for them. Every day I have to face a lot of problems when I go training. All along there have been people who wanted to disturb me, to stop me," Kohistani said. "Coming to the Olympics was one of my dreams. It's more than eight years that I am running." Kohistani added, "I hope the next generation of women will be proud of me and that they will never forget me. I want them to come and join me."[472]

What Today's Women Are Thinking Should Change in Afghanistan?

Mentioned above are some of the developments those have taken place over the past decade. In the mentioned time span several developments have taken place across Afghanistan, these are just a few among them which can be seen as voices of Afghan women who have played their part in encouraging others. The position of women in the country was not determined over a course of a decade therefore it could never be expected that their status will change significantly in a course of few years. The family oriented patriarchal, paternalistic society in which gender roles have been clearly defined, men have been providing the wherewithal for survival and have been dealing with the world outside the home, while women nurture those within it and pass on the society's values. Family is the heart of Afghan society and the belief in male superiority provides the ideological basis for the acceptance of certain type male dominance deemed necessary to guarantee the integrity of the family.[473] "Boys are their parent's future. They are the ones who stick around and take care of their mothers, while girls are traded off to serve others. Girls to many are transients, so it does not pay to take too much notice of them or to grow attached. Empathy is unknown"- described a young Afghan girl when asked about what she feels girls in Afghanistan mean according to her.[474] Even in warm and loving families, girls occupy a peculiar and precarious psychic space and apparently that is dependent upon their good behaviour.[475] The way girls are welcomed into life helps explain why so many are willing to leave it. Ann Jones, writes about her encounter with a young lady doctor at Rabia Balkhi Hospital who angrily said to her:

> "You come here and ask me about violence and suicide, but you do nothing about it. I tell you in Farsi. I tell you in Pashtu. I tell you in English. They are dying everyday, these girls. They are beaten. Raped. Mutilated. What is needed is a central hospital for women victims of violence of all kinds, because there is no end to it...We give them psychological help, legal help. We help them find a way to live. Otherwise what can I do? I fix them up and send them back to the same husband or father or mother in law who beats them, rapes them and burns them again. No one keeps a record, there are many many cases, but they are lost."[476] The doctor adds "This is not politics, this is not one regime- Karzai, Taliban or Rabbani. This is patriarchy."

Human Rights investigators estimated that 95 percent of Afghan women are subjected to violence but the most important fact is that Afghani women believe that husbands by right will determine their sex life, they believe that husbands, mother-in laws by right can beat them at any time they want and fathers by right can kill them if they bring shame to their family, expressed an Afghan women working for an International NGO in Kabul. "If WE think like that, what change the world can possibly bring to Afghan women" she added.[477] Young educated girls of Kabul university, who might be expected to dispute this allotment of rights ask instead "what else can we do?".

Education is both a cornerstone for building Afghan women's human capital and a sine qua non for their equal enjoyment of rights and participation in national development. However, their access to a safe academic environment which can guarantee this is often beset with numerous constraints GBV is one such constrains. Gender Studies Department of Kabul University, conducted a research[478] at three of Afghanistan's premier educational Institutes (University of Kabul, Balkh and Herat) in 2010 gave an detailed and shocking picture about GBV at elite institutes in Afghanistan. Gender based violence, particularly sexual violence, happens to be a serious, life-threatening protection issue, primarily affecting women and children. Like in most other countries in Afghanistan also, it stems from power inequalities and asymmetries in society. While the Afghan Constitution maintains that men and women are equal before the law (Constitution Articles: 22 also see Articles 44, 53, 54, 83 and 84), there is a large gap between what is pronounced in writing and the reality. The findings of the research indicate that responsiveness to GBV and prevention mechanisms at Kabul University were limited with the majority of staff unaware of how to respond to incidents of GBV. One respondent claimed that "the university is neither capable of tackling GBV nor can it respond to the needs of students who have experienced GBV."[479] The report of GBV-related incidents at Balkh University, such as verbal abuse and physical harassment, on campus showed that it was prevalent on campus despite a lack of full understanding of the actual concept. While the Herat University campus is new and offers good facilities, many of female staff and students were not satisfied with the ability of the university to respond to and address their needs as women. Overall, the researchers reported that the female staff and students who were interviewed did not share the enthusiasm their male counterparts shared. One female member of staff stated that "what is lacking at the university is a climate of freedom".[480] In all the three universities the research finding was that there was no clear understand about what GBV was.

Yet the study conducted highlighted at few key finding, which indicated girls are subjected to verbal abuse in these universities. Some of them felt they are treated as 'second class citizens' within the campus. Photographing women against their consent and making abusive or degrading remarks are common in these elite institutes in Afghanistan. What and how people dress are considered to be a major factor in inviting GBV. Women were largely held responsible for inviting GBV by what they wear and how they present themselves, including by the other women. A reluctance to report these incidents can be noticed and these incidents mostly remain a matter of discussion in friend's circles. Kabul University is by far the most prestigious co-ed educational institute of the country where the student from reasonably elite backgrounds tend to get enrolled. Even there one can hardly find girls interacting with boys. Girls tend to move in all girls groups and maintain their distances from the boys. During an informal group discussion with some of the girls they shared the reason. Palwarsha, a B.A first year student said "Boys aren't good. It is better for us that we maintain safe distance from them." Another girl said that for a very brief period of time mixing with boys were encouraged at the university but the result was not "dangerous", as for the first time in the history of Kabul University "there was a rape case in the University". The situation went out of control and the Karzai government apparently had to intervene and mixing was stopped once again.[481] If this was the picture in a country's most premier educational institute, which is almost an elite hub, the situation of women in other spheres are easily understandable.

There are thousands of women in Afghanistan today who cannot even imagine a world in which decisions are held in the hands of women. Ministers at MOWA, themselves have publicly described beating of women as a "normal custom" in Afghanistan.[482] Ann Jones book writes about a young educated girl named Marzia, who vehemently opposes the view that women should not be arrested from sexual offence during a discussion. "We must have strong laws against Zina," Marzia Says, "otherwise men will not feel safe in allowing their wives and daughters to go out to work."[483] In the year 2004, an international agency investigated the women's prison in more conservative Herat and found that 78 percent of the women detained there were changed with Zina but in Pashtun majority provinces like Jalalabad, there were not a single cases of Zina. The officials explained that to the investigators conducting the research that such "problems" were handled "in the family." This was the inescapable burden of Afghan girls and women- the family honor.[484]Under the terms of 'tradition' and of 'Islamic' practices that 'protect' them, girls and women had to come to bear responsibility of moral life and reputation of the families that owned them. It is unknown how many girls and women, who apparently has brought shame upon the family, have been killed by their fathers and brothers or have been driven to suicide. Honor killing is not restricted among Afghans living in Afghanistan, Afghan immigrant families in western have been involved in such activities. In 2008, a Morsal Obeidi, the 16 year young girl in her teens in Germany was killed by her brother.[485] While the Obeidis were not an overtly conservative family the friction between the family and the rebellious teenager appeared to stem from her comfort with her 'western' lifestyle, a life she watched her peers have, which included uncovered hair, makeup and short skirts. The term 'honour killing' is controversial in itself, in that it places the burden of the family's honour and reputation on women – and girls as young or younger than Morsal - paving the way for their further victimisation.

Difference between these women and women from western societies or even some progressive societies arises from what their respective societies believe and teach through the law. Even in India, most of the people believe that wife beating is wrong. All through years of feminist political agitations were required to persuade the public opinion, it is now reflected in laws that criminalize rape, domestic violence, trafficking, forced prostitution, GBV etc and in other laws that mandate social supports for women victims of violence. But in Afghanistan, majority of the people seem to believe that men are superior creatures who have every right to do exactly as they please. An educated Afghan gentleman, who is currently finishing his Doctoral Research in a foreign country, in her posh bungalow at the Kabul City centre Shahr-e-Naw put across his point extremely comfortably.

"The fact the women today are 'trying' to establish they are equal to men indicated they are not. I must say Afghan women are more sensible in this respect, they know it is 'silly' to imagine that they are equal to men." In the question of marriage he expressed his faith in arranged marriage, like most respected Afghan men, his logic was simple, "love marriages don't work in my society, the girl who can get involved with me before marriage, who knows she might have other relationships as well...they can never be trusted!" Once questioned on the issue of multiple marriage he expressed in his broken Hindustani "*Agar bibi bachha nehi de sakta to 'bechara' kya kar sakta hain?Shaadi hi to karega na?...Socho agar biwi bimaar rehta hai, banda jo chahta hain wo nahi de saktu to bechara kya karega? Shaadi ke siwa who kya karega?*"[486] (If a wife cant be a motherwhat can the helpless husband do? Why wont he get married? If the wife is sick and fail to give him what he wants, what can possibly the pool husband do? What option does he have apart from remarriage?) However he was careful to add that it is very important for men that they take care of all their wives.

Ann Jones writes that in Afghan culture, marriage itself can become a kind of violence.[487] It may begin with the forced marriage of a child bride like that of the girl Osama in the movie- and a forced consummation that leaves the girl torn and permanently incapacitated. *The New York Times* reported a story of a young girl Sahar Gul, who refused to prostitute herself or have sex with the man she was forced to marry when she was about 13. The report says she was tortured by her in laws who threw her into a dirty, windowless cellar for months until the police discovered her lying in hay and animal dung.[488] As more details of Sahar Gul's case have come to light - including the fact that the abuse continued even as, time and again, neighbours, police officers and her family members voiced suspicions that something was wrong - it has only reinforced how vulnerable women and girls still are in Afghanistan, particularly in rural areas where under-age marriages are common and forced ones are typical.

Many of the young Kabuli brides are brought to hospitals for repairs the morning after their wedding night, and some of them die. Since hardly anyone keeps track of birth dates or marriages, it is difficult to gather statistics of child marriages, in countryside especially it seems to be rampant even today. Poor families counting on a bride price do well to sell a girl off early, before she is matured. The Afghan law today requires boys to b eighteen and girls at least sixteen to marry and Sharia calls for girls to be fifteen, however these laws, in most cases, like many other remain restricted to books. As Nazia, a working girl who has decided not to marry anyone gives an interesting reasoning behind not abiding by the law. "There are fundamentalists who believe in emulation Prophet, they point out that the Prophet himself married a girl who was nine year old. In countryside girls of seven and eight years are brides.[489]

In Kabul Nazia adds that the midwives who serve the poorest neighbourhoods sometimes find child brides locked up or even chained, so that they do not run away. Nazia had earlier expressed her aversion for marriage citing that "my society does not produce men who can be married", it did appear to be a strong statement not only in the context of Afghan society but many others as well but the reasons behind such stand made her claims legitimate.

Ann Jones writes in her book that at Kabul's famous Malalai Hospital, seventy plus women give birth everyday. Hospital source informs the author only about 5 percent of husbands permit contraception.[490] It is common to find child brides unconscious or asleep in the recovery ward of the hospital. These girls, Jones writes or eleven or twelve, are still children, their bodies still underdeveloped to give birth.[491] Such young girls are likely to bear malnourished, defective and retarded babies, babies that cannot thrive. The Doctors informed the author that they have noticed a curious thing about the child brides, "They do not bond with their babies, it is as if they feel nothing".[492] Situations of girls who burn themselves are worst. The doctor at the hospital explains the circumstances in which girls decide to kill themselves. When they get married, it is expected that the girls must bleed at their wedding night or else people will say they are bad girls and beat them and put them out of house. These girls are often too scared to go back to their father's house so they decide to burn themselves. However the real reason never comes out, as the girls themselves site "accident" as reason of their burn. Sometimes hospital stuffs report suspicious cases to the police, but unfortunately the police also do not take much interest in these cases of what they called "kitchen victims". Things are changing very slowly, in exceptional cases the government tend to take actions. Sahar

Gul's case, for example drew attention from President Hamid Karzai and the international news media, is the exception that proves the rule: a small victory that masks a still-depressing picture of widespread instances of abuse of women that never come to light.[493] With her mistreatment a big story in the Afghan news media, President Karzai called for swift justice. In a district court in Kabul on May 1, the judge, speaking in front of a bank of microphones on national television, declared Sahar Gul's three in-laws guilty.[494]

It is not that women don't have their tricks, they have to manipulate their moves to get through the day; "they have their little illness and their little rivalries and their little gossips. They can throw knives around a corner" observed Afghan German Tamina[495], but these were essentially subvertive tactics of people who know they have zero real power. The women in Afghanistan are brainwashed from their childhood. University Professor Nahid Rashimi shared her experience, "when men are in the room, the girl students don't speak up. They don't answer questions. I cant blame them. I donot speak myself if I am in a meeting or discussion with my male colleagues, I am always careful not to say too much and even when I want to make a point, I am always careful not to say too much"[496] Sheila and Massouda works for one of the most renowned think tanks of Afghanistan. They have worked in several important research projects and claim that their office environment is "much better" that most of other offices in the country. However, during their lunch break, Sheila and Massouda quietly goes out in the garden and eats separately. There is a cook who cooks meal for the male colleagues, but they are different, they are women, perhaps among the few progressive women in the country yet they feel "it is ok" for their male colleges not to invite them for the treats they give to others in the organization.[497] One of them appeared to be an excellent orator, when asked why she doesn't participate in conferences organized in other countries, she expressed "even if I want to I wont be allowed to go. Neither by my family nor my organization." She added, "If I manage to go and speak my mind, I will face a lot of problem once I came back to Afghanistan...so its better that I don't go."[498] Ann Jones shares her experience of attending several conferences on issues pertaining to women in Afghanistan with minimal female representation in them and discusses about how Afghan men saw women and women's issues. Her experience at The National Conference on Women's Rights, law and Justice in Afghanistan hosted in May 2003 by International Human Rights Law Group and sponsored by UNIFEM and Government of Germany and Italy was particularly interesting, as she spoke about a women professor of law from Kabul University (in the audience) bravely pointed to a all male panel speaking on Women's rights in reference to Quran said that " The pen that records the rights of women is always held in the hand of a man". The men laughed. She added: "the pen that recorded the Holy Quran was held in the hand of man." The men stopped laughing, and in the chastening silence the followed she sank into the chair, writes Jones.[499]In the same two-day conference the eminent jurists sited women's "three day sickness" to prove that they are lesser creatures unworthy of Human Rights. When the author asked the female participant that why are they saying "three" when the number is more than that, she responded by saying "if they know the true number of days we are 'polluted', they would busy us alive."[500] By the time the conference was over, it was clear to the author that lot of other information eluded the most eminent jurists in Afghanistan.

Despite having 25 percent of the parliamentary seats filled by women, the parliament has approved a controversial amnesty law, calling for immunity for all those involved in war-time violations of human rights and women's rights; approved the Shiite Personal Status Law, subjecting Shiite women to traditional religious controls which later on was reviewed and amended to some extent; and pointedly did not approve presidential nominees for the position of minister of women's affairs.[501] The Asia Foundation Survey showed,25% of the total respondents identified lack of education or illiteracy as the biggest problem faced by Afghan women in 2011, followed by lack of rights (15%), domestic violence (9%), poverty, forced marriage and health care (8% each).[502] According to Womankind Worldwide, a UK charity, 80% of Afghan women are affected by domestic violence, over 60% of marriages are forced, and half of all girls are married before the age of 16.[503] According to a 2008 Violence Against Women Primary Database Report from UNIFEM, in Afghanistan, women and girls are mostly abused by people close to them; i.e. family members (father, mother, brother(s), sister(s), life partners (husband, fiancée, ex-husband and/or boyfriend), step family members, in-laws and other relatives). This group amounts to 92% of the reported cases of abuse. [504] Frequently, "when the women or girls seek recourse from the government they are further molested by the government representatives."[505] Inspite of improved representation of women in Afghan public life, gender based violence and inequities remain inherent. There is an increasing belief in Afghanistan that issues like undermining of justice, inadequate transparency and accountability from the government, corruption, impunity from crimes committed by powerful influential figures, half hearted international effort are major reasons for the country's current chaos and widespread insecurity. Regardless of the main causes, it was felt that reconciliation and negotiation could produce a solution to a violent conflict and accordingly steps were taken that ultimately culminated into 'Qatar Process' in early 2012. However the key question for Afghan women remained: reconciliation, and especially reintegration, at what cost?

Perceived Threats of Afghan Women beyond 2014

With the deadline for international troops withdrawal in 2014 getting closer and the Taliban strength display on a rise, majority of Afghan women are becoming concerned about their future. Some of them are conscious about the realities and challenges which my sweep the country after 2014, an intensifying sense of uneasiness is palpable among women today. "I am not optimistic about the future in general and especially as a woman" said a lady doctor from Mazar-e-Shariff, as she feels that security and economic situation will worsen once troops leave Afghanistan.[506] A young Tajik girl, working in one of the most renowned Research organizations in Kabul was also apprehensive about the future for a different reason. She expressed "Afghans have always worked better and collectively against a perceived enemy...think of British, Russian and now Americans, now once US leave, they would not have that 'enemy' to fight against, therefore they will start fighting against each other and civil war is the last thing that this country can afford at this moment."[507] When enquired about the future of women in general, some of the working women interviewed expressed, "things don't look too good, it's quite possible that we'll be compelled to leave our jobs and lead a restricted life...it is so 'scary' to even think of what is awaiting us."[508] Girls at Kabul University campus responding on the issue of gender discrimination and gender based violence argued, "Why 2014? Even now University campus is not free from these...verbal, sexual abuses, harassment are very much a part of our reality today, so it is pointless to think about post 2014 situation."[509] Naheed Farid, a member of the National Assembly from Herat, says that post-2014 Afghanistan poses serious threats to women's rights with the potential for increasing violence. "Afghan women will witness dangerous backsliding on their rights if the government does not take the necessary steps to ensure and defend women's rights after foreign troop withdrawal."[510] Janan Mosazai, Spokesperson of Afghanistan Foreign Ministry seemed a little more optimistic, as he cited the progress made in the past few years particularly in gender issues and believes that Afghanistan would need continued International backing to take the process forward and was confident that Afghanistan would receive the required support to fight such problems.[511] Unfortunately his sentiment was not shared by Tariq Sapi, father of three daughters from Kunar District. According to him, situations in provinces are starkly different from Kabul, "Taliban is stronger than government in my area, they are threatening families against sending their daughters to schools, there have been acid attacks on school going girls, under such circumstances, how can we send our girls to schools?"[512] The poisoning of drinking water at a High School in Kunduz Province, which resulted in the hospitalization of 150 girls in April 2012 also indicated strengthening of conservative radicals opposed to female education in the country.[513]

One of the most formidable obstacles faced by women in Afghanistan happens to be the deteriorating security situation. "Since 2006, suicide attacks have increased", observed a lady doctor from Afghanistan, who had come to Jaipur, India for to attend a Training programme. Human Rights Watch 2007 has also indicated that since 2006, the attacks increased sic fold from the previous year and bombing and arson attacks on schools in Afghanistan doubled.[514] Afghans in general are caught between a weak, often predatory government and anti government faction that use coercion, terror and violence to secure control. In the interviews carried out with several Afghan women at the beginning of April 2012, many of them shared about the difference between the security situation in Kabul and the near by areas where Taliban was increasingly gaining control. Meena, a working girl from Kabul even said, "you don't have to go too far, go 3 kilometers outside Kabul and you will see a different picture...but I wound obviously not want you to go there and experience the hell!"[515] With in a few days after interaction with Meena, an interesting observation came out from a group discussion with a few working women at a renowned Research Organization in Kabul. One of them claimed that she had been observing some unusual movements within Kabul itself, while she spoke the others present in the discussion seconded her observation. When enquired more on the matter she said "going by my sixth sense, my suspicion is that there would a major Taliban offensive with a month...I didn't observe these movements (in Kabul) for quite some times now, hope I am wrong".[516] Shockingly with ten days after the conversation, the most dramatic and widespread attack took place in the Afghan capital. Taliban spokes person termed the multiple and simultaneous attacks in several sites of Kabul and provinces like Paktia, Logar and Nangarhar as "Taliban Spring Offensive".[517] The objective was to let the world know that Taliban was strong enough to attack at will the most sensitive installations in best guarded parts of the capital. After the attack when the same lady was asked that when she as a commoner could anticipate something like this, how could the political dispensation be taken aback after the attack?, the lady laughed and remarked "If our government was an efficient one we would not have been in the position where we are today."[518] Some of the Afghans interviewed after the attacks expressed their pride on the way Afghan Security Forces had fought the insurgents during that attack and how they expected the Karzai government to take a strong position by condemning the attack. To much of their disappointment, President Karzai instead of taking a condemning the insurgents and applauding the bravery of the Security Forces, apparently said in an interview given to their National Television, that the Taliban's were his brothers and urged them to join the Reconciliation and Reintegration Process.[519] During several occasions women (essentially non Pashtuns) had expressed how people have lost confidence in President Karzai, some of them even questioned his "mental health" over course of interviews. One girl even said, "Karzai is funny and even now he is trying his best to be in 'good books' of all people", she added, "when he gives a speech, he starts in Dari then moves to Pashtu and then again to Dari and then he always makes it appoint to use some Uzbek-i words in his speech...so that people don't alienate from him". When asked what was the problem in his approach considering he is the President of a multi-ethnic nation? The girl promptly responded, "the problem is, his 'fair' intentions are limited only to Speeches".[520]

Considering mostly Tajik and Hazara women came out to work and persue a career in the change environment after 2001, the women interviewed for the study essentially have been non-Pashtuns, with an exception of a few. Most of them were pessimistic about the situation beyond 2014. "Today while the International security forces are very much in the country, if the situation is like this, then the situation once they leave would be anybody's guess" expressed Simin, a Tajik girl currently working at a private company in Kabul.[521] They feel that the little voice or position that they have in their families are because of their monetary contribution in the family, "though we have ask permission about certain things from our unemployed brothers, but still we feel we are in a much better position but unfortunately this too will change after 2014. Some expressed that they are pretty certain the Talban will come back (may not be immediately) and their movement would be restricted once again. Some of women expressed that, the Taliban in the old 'avatar' is unlikely to come back, they would atleast 'pretend' of adopting a moderate position on issues of gender, however in reality they might remain the way they were. They feel this would be important and convenient for all. Marriam explained, " the international community (read America) justified the attack on Afghanistan in terms of liberation of the women. Everybody knows their only aim was to catch Osama and show their people that the strongest nation has taken revenge of the embarrassment of 9/11. Now after more than ten years of experience in Afghanistan, they are impatient to leave the country even in a situation when the terrorism, insurgency, human rights violation in the country are on the rise. But for them it is convenient to shut eyes to these at this moment. Their efforts at appealing to Taliban through Qatar Process is an indication that they tried to pursue Taliban to adopt a relatively 'moderate position' on certain issues (like gender) that would make it easy for them to welcome Taliban back in Kabul...they are anyway 'tired' with Karzai".[522]

Many Afghans in Kabul expressed that they are waiting for the first opportunity to migrate from Afghanistan. Some of the women interviewed expressed that their families are thinking of migrating to other countries. Germany, Canada, Australia and India appeared to be most coveted destinations for resettlements for them. It is quite likely that beyond 2014, there would be a third wave of migration from Afghanistan and many countries would feel the pressure of Afghan refugees seeking asylum that was experienced in the past during Soviet intervention and Taliban regime. Some of the women expressed that they or their families are contacting their relatives and friends who are settled in other countries to know if they can migrate and settle there as they feel Afghanistan will cease to be a 'liveable place' beyond 2014 especially for non Pashtuns. They feel Pashtuns are in a way welcoming the withdrawal as they know, once Taliban comes back they will adopt a more favourable attitude towards Pahtuns and they would be happy to see people from their ethnicity in again in control of political power in Afghanistan the way it has always been. A girl jokingly said, "whenever their is a Taliban attack we tease out Pashtun colleges saying that its by their 'brothers'...they get embarrassed. It is true that not all Pashtuns support Talibans as they have also been victims of Taliban acts but in reality some where they have a soft corner because they belong to same ethnicity.[523]

Most of the women today in Afghanistan feel that perhaps the greatest challenge to the country is the lack of political will. They feel conference after conference, statements after statements have articulated a long commitment to Afghanistan and to the people of the country yet the Donors actions on ground have created serious doubts. International community's expectations of what could be achieved in Afghanistan were only a shadow of what they were just a few years ago. As UK Defence Minister Liam Fox had remarked: "We are not in Afghanistan for the sake of the education policy in a broken 13th century country. We are there so the people of Britain and our global interest are not threatened.[524] Another foreign official commented: "Afghanistan will never be Switzerland, but perhaps ten or twenty years from now it can be like Bangladesh".[525] Such vague and patronizing definitions of "success", together with the increasing unpopularity of war in troop contributing countries and pressure to "show results" have contributed to an over emphasis on military objectives and militarised solutions in Afghanistan. However it is important to remember that there have been concrete improvements on the lives of many Afghan women, it is just that they have fallen short of expectations and are being reversed by insecurity in some areas.

CONCLUSION

> "This is my country, my future and my children's future: I have no hope but to hope. There will be peace here one day but when this happens, I cannot control. I can only put my faith in Allah and hope for those with the power to gain a conscience"
>
> – An women school teacher from Kabul, Afghanistan[526]

The objective behind a research on Afghan women across a broad spectrum of almost a century was to study the transition they had experienced in those years. With the review of the experiences of Afghans over the years and by listening to Afghan women's voices that we can begin to understand the struggle for their identity, rights and recognition. By standards of many societies in this world the developments which have been termed as 'achievements' for gender related issues in Afghanistan might appear to be insignification, something that doesn't even deserve recognition, but once compared with the scenarios and experiences of the past, the impacts can be evaluated. Therefore, an attempt has been made to review the position enjoyed by women in the remote past (*Yesterday)*, starting from the monarchies up to the present generation of women (*Today*) and also what they feel the future generations of women are likely to face in Afghanistan in the days after the withdrawal of International Forces in 2014 (*Tomorrow*).

Afghanistan has always had elite and middle class women who asserted their rights and marched towards modernization. Those women who were publicly visible throughout the history of Afghanistan belonged to the royalty or elite and represented a very tiny population of the country. They did act as role models and provided a window into the possibility that social change can occur and illustrated the potential that women from different strata of society can attempt change in their lives even in Afghanistan. But despite these examples, the majority of Afghan women in rural areas have not been able to identify with them because they were experiencing strict tribal customs and dictates in their everyday life. There has always remained a huge gap between the experiences and expectations of Afghan women from rural and urban areas. Though the country's majority of female population resides in rural areas and share beliefs and aspirations much different from their urban counter parts, hardly any attempt has been made to listen to their voices. One obvious obstacle remain the limited access but inspite of that handicap, an important aim of this research has been to throw light at the situation of Afghan women in rural across generations.

For majority of Afghan women, rural and urban, now and in the past, the family has functioned as paramount social institution and the primary obligation for them has been to uphold family honour by conforming to accepted behavioural norm. Afghan society has always been strictly patriarchal and the male dominance for women have been impossible to escape. Non conformist behaviour on part of women, on the other hand, heralded social disorder and threatened the duel concept of male honor and family status. The idea has been therefore, women must be protected and kept inviolable. Community pressures have often become a powerful force in perpetuating customs such as restrictive seclusion, limit of freedom of movement, denial of education and exclusion from public forums, even though these constraints expressed male values that refute the Islamic concept of a dignified life for all. As eminent expert on Afghanistan Nancy Dupree has observed, untangling the contradictions between Islamic dicta and practice has always been challenging especially so today when conservative militants project rights for women as an external ideology linked to foreign invasions threatening male honor and contaminating Afghan values. [527] The voices of religious hierarchy who dare speak out on the consequence of early marriages, gender based abuses, advocates of education, the right to work, spaced pregnancies, condoms, breast feedings and immunizations, confirm the compatibility of a whole range of human rights with the tenets of Islam. The impact of these messages of spreading in Afghanistan.[528] Through this research we've seen that a wide diversity of attitudes have governed male-female relationships in Afghanistan depending on the region, rural or urban setting and education levels. While a belief in the fitness of male authority predominates among all groups, gender equity tended to be more amicably practiced in rural households where interconnectedness of male and female economic activities tended to build respect through bonds of partnership. History reminds us that gender is an issue that takes long time to mature. The pressures to produce instant results seems to be unrealistic, especially now in Afghanistan when politician grapple with deteriorating domestic and international confidence.

In the past decade significant progress on women's rights in Afghanistan have been achieved, a testament to the hard work of activists and policy makers. A robust gender polity framework has been established. The Convention on the Elimination of All Forms of Discrimination against women have been ratified and the new Constitution guarantees gender equality and secures specific rights for women such as 25% of seats in Parliament, provincial councils and district assemblies. The National Action Plan for the Women of Afghanistan, a national framework for gender equity, has been adopted. Numbers reveal that impact of these policies: 2.5 million girls now attend school, women constitute a quarter of the members of Parliament and about 30,000 women have formal voices of community councils. Heartening new developments indicate that many men once willing to support women's efforts privately are now doing so publicly. These changes have been linked to the fact that women at all levels learned to cope alone with sets of new experiences during years of war and displacement. Their roles expanded, their leadership skills sharpened in many respects women became agents of change. They have proven by their capabilities that they can function in public with no loss of honour to themselves, to their family or to society. This fact is much widely accepted today. With such supports women have forged ahead in the past decade. Women have successfully thwarted attempts to cut the number of seats allocated for women in Parliament, called for and won places at major forums from which they were initially excluded and contributed to major debates. On another crucial level of governance women are slowly accepting opportunities to work with men on Provincial and District Councils, which has been a great achievement in itself.

Elsewhere women, inside Burqa or out, have been engaged in every sector, at family counselling centers as lawyers and social workers, as doctors, nurses, teachers and health workers, as judges, as business women small and large, as engineers and architects; as IT specialists; as journalists, writers, researchers and entertainers in the arts, in the theatre, in radio and TV; as Foreign service officers, policewomen, army officers and as civil servants of all sorts, including a governor, ministers and directors of commissions.[529] Although for women, motherhood remains priority in life. Those women who are pursuing careers in Afghanistan today, are expected to balance both home and professional fronts like their counterparts in rest of the world.

Despite these gains progress remains fragile. Many gaps remain. Afghanistan still has one of the highest mortality rates in the world. Illiteracy among adult women is 88% and only 6% of women over 25 have formal educations. Social restrictions exist that impede the mobility of women and deny them the right to work, inherit and own land. Pervasive violence against women and girls still pose serious threats to their lives and block them for reaching their potential. Several reports have indicated that majority of women in the country experience at least one form of violence of forced marriage in their lifetime. Afghan women still struggle to participate in a meaningful way in political dialogues. Despite efforts, women's empowerment at the grassroots level has not yet materialized. Lack of security hampers women's return to active social and political life. Poverty continues to make the lives of women refugees and war widows miserable. The violence and crime against women remain high. Seeking justice still remains tedious for a number of women due to weakness in the criminal justice system.

Biases and prejudices continues to exist against women even within judiciary and parliament. Health and education of women remains abysmally low both due to lack of will and lack of ability to seek both. Warlords and criminals enjoy vast powers threatening security situation and interfering in the fair execution of justice system. The government has failed to provide even minimal security to Afghan women as the crime in most cases go unpunished. The lack of genuine will and commitment to improve women's lives on the part of the government and the international community has been observed which is indicative of the fact that the invasion was more about strategic interest that about liberating the oppressed women of Afghanistan. Patriarchal attitudes against women lie at the root of the discrimination faced by women. Understanding of and respect for Afghan religion and culture is required in order to initiate enduring, meaningful reform within the system. Reforms cannot be imposed from outside. The government and its international partners put dealing with terrorism and security issues as their prime priority and preoccupation, which has eclipsed the pertinence of women's issues and has led to slackening of effort on this front. The lives of Afghan women today, after decade of international support and billions of dollars of aid have not significantly improved. The following section attempts to put forward a few recommendations, many of which have been made before by several individuals and organizations, yet have largely fallen on deaf ears. 2012 is a decisive year for Afghanistan, as perhaps every year has been since 2002. But as time passes, the window of opportunity to correct the course of action seems to become smaller and smaller. This may be the last chance to do things right by the Afghan people and the world community. Given the fragile security situation, failure to do so risks pushing the country towards even greater levels of conflict and devastation. It is true that many around the world are pessimistic about the prospects in Afghanistan- except, seemingly, many Afghans like the female teacher from Kabul quoted above.

While the government's efforts to improve sub-national governance and create "bankable" programs are essential to address the underlying causes of crises and help Afghan lift themselves out of poverty, they are far from sufficient. A fundamental change in donor thinking and a new found political will and continued support to the existing government beyond the period of 2014 is required.

Recommendations

- Policy needs to be matched with implementation. Constitutional reform will only be effective if the criminal justice system and state institutions to administer it are reformed.
- Corruption of funds for women's development programmes by state officials and NGOs must be checked and effectively stemmed.
- Criminal elements in the administration needs to be flushed out. An independent inquiry of criminal past record of influential warlords and functionaries must be carried out and legal punishments accorded. Crime against women will not stop unless its influential sponsors are taken to task.
- All parties to the conflict in Afghanistan must abide by the commitment to observe international human rights and humanitarian law guaranteeing the protection of civilians, and to investigate and hold accountable military personnel responsible for violations. In particular, the U.S.-led alliance must ensure that human rights and humanitarian law is not violated in any circumstances.
- It must be ensured that development and reconstruction programs are structured to ensure that girls and women have full access to programs for education, health care, job training and housing.
- The international community must ensure that any government established in Afghanistan is committed to fully respect the human rights of all the people of Afghanistan and to repealing laws and ending practices that discriminate against women.
- Police reforms and training must be carried out. More women need to be recruited in the police service.

- Women's access to justice through smaller courts in rural areas must be facilitated. More women must be recruited into the judiciary.
- Registration of marriage and divorce, as well as accurate entry of birth records must be made compulsory and any breach should be punishable.
- Laws regarding the legal age of marriage must be strictly implemented.
- Awareness of family laws, marriage and divorce laws must be created among women through education and the media.
- Rehabilitation centres for women must be increased and made approachable.
- Widows and orphans as well as despondent women must receive monthly stipends in aid from international donors and NGOs through the Ministry of Women's Affairs.
- More health centres providing reproductive health services for women should be established, especially in far-flung rural areas.
- Female staffs must be recruited into the health system.
- Training must be imparted to women for basic and emergency health services.
- Training to develop skills must be given to women to encourage them to work from home.
- Entrepreneurial skills should be taught to women to help them acquire independent means of earning.
- Domestic violence must be made legally punishable.
- More girls schools need to be established, especially in rural areas.
- Security must be provided in schools and strict action taken against those who threaten girl students.
- Religious leaders should be recruited to promote women's education and rights in the light of religion. Arrangements

should be made to impart such education through religion to the public, men and women alike.

- International NGOs avoid advocating imposition of secular Western law, but help reform the system from within. They need to build trust among the people through respect of ancient values and traditions.
- Misunderstanding regarding religious law should be dispelled, and awareness of its correct and progressive interpretation needs to be spread through the media.
- Religion must be delinked from false notions of 'honour and shame' and gender apartheid.
- The media must not present the liberation of women cosmetically through the ornamentalization and exposure of women, but should play a proactive role in public education about women's rights.
- Edicts handed down by local jirgas needs to be licensed and approved by the Afghanistan Supreme Court.
- Discriminatory laws needs to be amended or repealed altogether.
- Gender issues must be accorded priority by the government and the international community.

Today Kabul looks and feels different from what it must have been at the time of the Taliban. There are beauty salons for women, nightclubs, music shops and entertainment venues in abundance. However, side by side, the quiet life of impoverished women begging on the streets goes on. Things are not nearly as good in the rural areas. The 'burqa' is still very much around as integral to Afghan culture. While many women visit the parlours and clubs, most simply cannot afford to, or are not interested, while they worry about their daily battle to survive. These hallmarks of liberation are largely cosmetic and there are few women who actually relish the fruits of liberation. For most others, it is still an elusive dream.

To conclude, it can be said that since 2001 Afghan women and girls have taken great personal risks to renegotiate the rigid gender roles and identities imposed upon them by tradition and Taliban. Afghan attitudes towards women, their roles and their economic, social and political participation have evolved over generations. The tectonic shifts required to achieve gender equity was never meant to come overnight and thus will require long-term commitment from the Afghan government, civil society, the international community and Afghans themselves. In the past decade, with the support of international community Afghan women have catalyzed change in many sectors; although their overall condition remains difficult. Indeed, women are the people upon whom a lasting solution depends, and their position in post-conflict Afghanistan will determine the course of the nation. Therefore it is very important for the international community to ensure that the steps taken forward by women of Afghanistan does not get halted, if it fails in that, it will speak very little about Afghan women but a great deal about themselves.

NOTES

1. Revolutionary Association of the Women of Afghanistan (RAWA), "Biography of Martyred Meena, Founding Leader of RAWA." http://imaginetoday.net/2009/01/20/radical-radiance-meena-keshwar-kamal/ (accessed on 24. 07. 2012)
2. Rashid, Ahmed, *Descent into Chaos, How the war against Islamic Extremism is being lost in Pakistan, Afghanistan and Central Asia,* Penguin Books, 2008.
3. Eleheh Rostami-Povey, *Afghan Women, Identity and Invasion,* zed Books, London and New York, 2007.
4. Nancy Hatch Dupree, "Veil In Afghanistan", *ASIA,* July/ August, 1978.
5. Nancy Hatch Dupree, "Veil In Afghanistan", *ASIA,* July/ August, 1978.
6. Ibid.
7. "Transition within Women: Restoring Women's Participation in Afghanistan", Conference Report from John F Kennedy School of government, Dec 7-9, Cambridge.
8. Peter Marsden, *The Taliban: War, Religion and the New Order in Afghanistan,* Oxford University Press, London, 1998, p.87.
9. Hafizullah Emadi, *Dynamics of Political Development in Afghanistan,* Palgrave Macmillan, 2010.
10. Jan Goodwin, *Price of Honour: Muslim Women Lift the Veil od Silence on the Islamic World,* Little Brown Publishers, Boston, 1994, p.77.
11. Ibid.
12. Arpita Basu Roy, *Contemporary Afghanistan, Conflict and Peace Building,* Har-anand Publication, 2010, p. 27.
13. Central Intelligence Agency, *The World Factbook, 2008. https://www.cia.gov/library/publications/the-world-factbook/*
14. Hafisullah Emadi, Op.cit.
15. Ibid.
16. Louis Dupree, *Afghanistan,* Oxford University Press, Karachi, Oxford, New York and Delhi, 1997, p.57.
17. Hafisullah Emadi, Op.cit., p.3.
18. Ibid, p.4.
19. Stephen Tanner, *Afghanistan: A Military History from Alexander The Great to the Fall of the Taliban,* De Capo Press, New York, 2002, p.1.
20. Arpita Basu Roy, Op.cot, p.26.
21. Louis Dupree, *Afghanistan,* Princeton University Press, Princeton, 1973, p.xii.
22. Ibid, p.30.
23. Arpita Basu Roy, Op.cit, p.31.
24. Ibid.
25. Ibid, p.59.

26. Hafizullah Emadi,Op.cit, p.2
27. Ahmed Rashid, *Descent into Chaos*, Penguin Press, London,pp. 265-266.
28. Donald N. Wilber, et al., *Afghanistan: Its People, Its Societies, Its Culture, HRAF Press, 1962, p.136.*
29. Huma Ahmed-Ghosh, "A History of Women in Afghanistan: Lessons Learn for the Future", *Journal for International Women's Studies*, Vol-4, May 2003.
30. Helen Hardacre, "The Impact of Fundamentalism on Women, the Family and Interpersonal Relations", in *Fundamentalisms and Society: Reclaiming the Scxiences, the Family and Education*, edited by Martin Marty and R Scott Appleby, University of Chicago Press, Vol.2, 1993, p.118.
31. Louis Dupree, *Afghanistan*, Princeton University Press, 1080, p. 531.
32. Huma Ahmed-Ghosh, A History of Women in Afghanistan: Lessons Learnt for the Future. Diss. San Diego State University, 2003. Print.
33. Ibid.
34. Emmanuel Todd, *The Explanation of ideaology: Family Structures and social systems*, Basil Blackwell Ltd., Oxford, England, 1985, pp-140-141.
35. Ibid.
36. Rosemarie Skaine, *The Women of Afghanistan Under the Taliban*, McFarland & Company, Inc., Publishers, London, 2002, pp.34-35.
37. Zeiba Shorish-Shamley, *Testimony*, Hearings, July 20, 2000 cited in Rosemarie Skaine, *The Women of Afghanistan Under the Taliban*, McFarland & Company, Inc., Publishers, London, 2002, pp.34-35
38. Ibid.
39. Ibid.
40. Interviews were carried with several Afghan men both in India and in Afghanistan by the author between 2011-2012.
41. Ibid.
42. Zeiba Shorish-Shamley, *Testimony*, Hearings, July 20, 2000 cited in Rosemarie Skaine, *The Women of Afghanistan Under the Taliban*, McFarland & Company, Inc., Publishers, London, 2002, pp.34-35
43. Abdul Raheem Yaseer was the Coordinator of International Exchange Programme and deputy director of the Centre for Afghanistan studies at University of Nebraska at Omaha.
44. Rosemarie Skaine, *The Women of Afghanistan Under the Taliban*, McFarland & Company, Inc., Publishers, London, 2002, pp.36-37.
45. "Transition within Tradition: Restoring Women's Participation in Afghanistan" John F Kennedy School of Governemnt Conference Paper, Cambridge, Massachusetts December 2001,
46. Ibid.
47. Rosemarie Skaine, Op.cit.
48. Zeiba Shorish-Shamley, *Testimony*, Hearings, July 20, 2000 cited in Rosemarie Skaine, *The Women of Afghanistan Under the Taliban*, McFarland & Company, Inc., Publishers, London, 2002, p. 37.

49. Sarah Alaoui, "Women's Status in Islam:The Line between Culture and Religion", *Journal for International Affairs,*Feb 2011. http://prospectjournal.ucsd.edu/index.php/2011/02/womens-status-in-islam-the-line-between-culture-and-religion/
50. Ibid.
51. Sarah Alaoui, "Women's Status in Islam:The Line between Culture and Religion", *Journal for International Affairs,*Feb 2011. http://prospectjournal.ucsd.edu/index.php/2011/02/womens-status-in-islam-the-line-between-culture-and-religion/
52. Bhutto, Benazir. "The Prophet Preached Equal Rights; Now the Task Is To Restore Them." Asiaweek 25 Aug. 1995.
53. IRIN Asia | AFGHANISTAN: Taliban Forces Students out of Schools into Madrasas | Asia | Afghanistan | Children Education Gender Issues Conflict | Feature." IRIN " Humanitarian News and Analysis from Africa, Asia and the Middle East – Updated Daily. Web. 11 Mar. 2010.
54. "'Poison attack' on 120 school girls in Afghanistan", *The Times of India,* 25th May, 2012.
55. Bhutto, Benazir. "The Prophet Preached Equal Rights; Now the Task Is To Restore Them." Asiaweek 25 Aug. 1995.
56. William Maley, "Introduction: Interpreting the Taliban" in William Maley (ed) *Fundamentalist Reborn? Afghanistan and the Taliban,* New York University Press, 1998, p.28.
57. Rosemarie Skaine, Op.cit, p.37.
58. Hassan Hathout, "Plight of Women in Afghanistan", *Islamic Intellectual Forum,* October 8, 2001
59. Hassan Hathout, "Plight of Women in Afghanistan", *Islamic Intellectual Forum,* October 8, 2001 in Rosemarie Skaine, *The Women of Afghanistan Under the Taliban,* McFarland & Company, Inc., Publishers, London, 2002, pp.36-37.
60. Muslim Woman's Leagues, "Crisis in Afghanistan", Nov, 1996.
61. Women Living Under Muslim Laws, "Increased Structural Violence", *Off our Backs 27,* no.3, March 1997, p.11.
62. Robert D Crew and Amin Tarzi (ed), "The Taliban and the Crisis of Afghanistan", Havard University Press, London, USA, 2008, p154.
63. Sarah Alaoui, "Women's Status in Islam:The Line between Culture and Religion", *Journal for International Affairs,*Feb 2011. http://prospectjournal.ucsd.edu/index.php/2011/02/womens-status-in-islam-the-line-between-culture-and-religion/
64. Ibid.
65. Sura Al-Nessa, *Al Qur'an* (4:124), http://www.masjidtucson.org/quran/noframes/ch4.html
66. Orzala Ashraf Nemat "Afghan Women: Agents of Peace- Or its Victim?"*A Century Foundation Report,* 2011.

67. Nancy Hatch Dupree, 1998b. *Afghan Women Under the Taliban* in William Maley (ed) Fundamentalism Reborn? Afghanistan and the Taliban, New York University Press.
68. Barakat, Sultan & Wardell, Gareth, "Capitalizing on Capabilities of Afghan Women: Women's Role in Afghanistan's Reconstruction and Development", *International Labour Organization*, CRISIS Working Paper4,Geneva, 2002, p.8.
69. Nancy Hatch Dupree, "Revolutionary Rhetoric and Afghan Women", *The Afghanistan Council-Asia Society*, Occasional Paper- 23, New York,1981,pp 1.3.
70. Ghosh Ahmed, Hume, "A History of Women in Afghanistan: Lessons Learn for the Future", *Journal of International Women's Studies*, Vol.4, May, 2003, p.1.
71. Nancy Hatch Dupree, *Women of Afghanistan*, Stiftung-Foundation, 1986.
72. Kakar, Hasan Kawun, *Government and Society in Afghanistan*, University of Texas Press, London, 1979, p.173.
73. Ghosh Ahmed, Huma, Op.cit.
74. Ibid, p.3.
75. Nancy Hatch Dupree, "Revolutionary Rhetoric and Afghan Women", *The Afghanistan Council-Asia Society*, Occasional Paper- 23, New York,1981,pp 1.3.
76. Magnus, Ralph H. and Eden Naby, *Afghanistan: Mullah, Marx and Mujahid*,Baulder: West view Press, 1998.
77. Schinasi, May, *Afghanistan at the beginning of the Twentieth Century: Nationalism and Journalism in Afghanistan-A Study by Seraj-ul-Akhbar (1911-1918)*, Instituto Universitario Orientale, Naples 1979.
78. Magnus, Ralph H. and Eden Naby, Op.cit, P.39.
79. Ghosh Ahmed, Huma, Op.cit, p.4.
80. Schinasi, Op.cit.
81. Nancy Hatch Dupree, "Revolutionary Rhetoric and Afghan Women", *The Afghanistan Council-Asia Society*, Occasional Paper- 23, New York,1981, p.1.
82. Olesen, Asta, *Islam and Politics in Afghanistan*, Curzon Press, Great Britain, 1996.
83. Magnus, Ralph H. and Eden Naby, Op.cit.
84. Ghosh Ahmed, Huma, Op.cit, p.4.
85. Dupree, N.H, "Revolutionary Rhetoric and Afghan Women", *The Afghanistan Council-Asia Society*, Occasional Paper- 23, New York,1981,p.1.
86. Ibid, p.2.
87. Ewans, Martin, *Afghanistan:A New History*, Curzon Press, 2001,p-94.
88. Ghosh Ahmed, Huma, Op.cit, p.5.
89. Ibid.
90. Hafizullah Emadi, *Dynamics of Political Development in Afghanistan: The British, Russian and American Invasions*, Palgrave Macmillan, 2010, p.27.

91. Ibid.
92. Ibid, p.27.
93. Ibid.
94. Ghosh Ahmed, Huma, Op.cit, p.5.
95. Ewans, Martin, *Afghanistan:A New History,* Curzon Press, 2001,p-94.
96. Moghadam, Valentine M., "Nationalist Agendas and Women's Rights: Conflicts in Afghanistan in Twentieth Century." In West, Louis A. (ed), *Feminist Nationalism.* Routledge, New York, 1997.
97. Ghosh Ahmed, Huma, Op.cit,p.6.
98. Ibid.
99. Nancy Hatch Dupree, "Revolutionary Rhetoric and Afghan Women", *The fghanistan Council-Asia Society,* Occasional Paper- 23, New York,1981,p.2.
100. Ibid.
101. Dupree, Louis., "The Burqa Comes Off", *American Universities Field Staff Report,* Vol-III, No.2 and *Afghanistan,* Princeton University Press, 1980, p.249.
102. Nancy Hatch Dupree, "Revolutionary Rhetoric and Afghan Women", *The Afghanistan Council-Asia Society,* Occasional Paper- 23, New York,1981,p.2.
103. Ibid.
104. Ghosh Ahmed, Huma, Op.cit,p.6.
105. Ibid, p.3.
106. Nancy Hatch Dupree, "Revolutionary Rhetoric and Afghan Women", *The Afghanistan Council-Asia Society,* Occasional Paper- 23, New York,1981,p.2.
107. Ghosh Ahmed, Huma, Op.cit,p.6.
108. Moghadam, Valentine M., " Nationalist Agendas and Women's Rights: Conflicts in Afghanistan in Twentieth Century" in West, Lois A. (ed) *Feminist Nationalism,* New York, Routledge, 1997.
109. Louis Dupree, *Afghanistan,* Princeton University Press, 1980.
110. Louis Dupree, "The Burqa Comes Off", *American Universities Field Staff Report,* Vol-III, No.2, 1980.
111. Yasgur, Batya Swift, *Behind the Burqa,* John Wiley and Sons Publishers, New Jersey, 2002, p.44.
112. Peter Marsden, *The Taliban: war and Religion in Afghanistan,* London, Zed Books, 2002.
113. Nancy Hatch Dupree, "Revolutionary Rhetoric and Afghan Women", *The Afghanistan Council-Asia Society,* Occasional Paper- 23, New York,1981, p.3.
114. Ibid.
115. Ibid.
116. Ghosh Ahmed, Huma, Op.cit, p.7.
117. Ibid.
118. Yasgur, Batya Swift, *Behind the Burqa,* John Wiley and Sons Publishers, New Jersey, 2002, p.185.
119. Zoya with Follain, John & Cristofari, Rita, *Zoya's Story,* Harper-Collins Publisher, New York, 2002.

120. Ghosh Ahmed, Huma, Op.cit, p.7.
121. Nancy Hatch Dupree, "Afghan Women Under the Taliban" in William Maley (ed) *Fundamentalist Reborn? Afghanistan and the Taliban,* New York University Press, 1998, p. 161.
122. Robert D. Crew and Amin Tarzi (ed), *The Taliban and the Crisis of Afghanistan,* Harvard University Press, London, USA, 2008, p.118.
123. Peter Marsden, *The Taliban :War, Religion and the New Order in Afghanistan,* Oxford University Press, London, 1998, pp. 98-99.
124. Aneela Sultana, "Taliban or Terrorist? Some reflection on Taliban's Ideology", *Politics and Religion Journal,* Vol-3, 2009,pp.7 – 24. http://www.politicsandreligionjournal.com/images/pdf_files/srpski/godina3_broj1/aneela%20sultana.pdf
125. Ibid
126. Robert D. Crew and Amin Tarzi (ed), *The Taliban and the Crisis of Afghanistan,* Harvard University Press, London, USA, 2008, p.118.
127. Ibid,p 126.
128. Jan Goodwin, "Buried Alive: Afghan Women under the Taliban", *On the Issue,*No.3, Summer 1998.
129. Peter Marsden, *The Taliban :War, Religion and the New Order in Afghanistan,* Oxford University Press, London, 1998, pp. 87-88.
130. Ibid.
131. Zoya with Follain, John & Cristofari, Rita, *Zoya's Story,* Harper-Collins Publisher, New York, 2002.
132. Robert D. Crew and Amin Tarzi (ed), *The Taliban and the Crisis of Afghanistan,* Harvard University Press, London, USA, 2008, p. 130.
133. Juan R. I. Cole, "The Taliban, Women, and the Hegelian Private Sphere", in Robert D. Crew and Amin Tarzi (ed), *The Taliban and the Crisis of Afghanistan,* Harvard University Press, London, USA, 2008, p. 131.
134. Ibid.
135. Juan R. I. Cole, "The Taliban, Women, and the Hegelian Private Sphere", in Robert D. Crew and Amin Tarzi (ed), *The Taliban and the Crisis of Afghanistan,* Harvard University Press, London, USA, 2008, p. 131.
136. Ibid, p. 133.
137. Juan R. I. Cole, "The Taliban, Women, and the Hegelian Private Sphere", in Robert D. Crew and Amin Tarzi (ed), *The Taliban and the Crisis of Afghanistan,* Harvard University Press, London, USA, 2008, pp. 135-136.
138. Ibid, p.137.
139. Ahmed Rashid, *Taliban,* Yale University Press, 2002.
140. Juan R. I. Cole, "The Taliban, Women, and the Hegelian Private Sphere", in Robert D. Crew and Amin Tarzi (ed), *The Taliban and the Crisis of Afghanistan,* Harvard University Press, London, USA, 2008, pp. 140-141.
141. Ibid, p.143.
142. Peter Marsden, *The Taliban :War, Religion and the New Order in Afghanistan,* Oxford University Press, London, 1998, pp. 95-98

143. Peter Marsden, *The Taliban :War, Religion and the New Order in Afghanistan,* Oxford University Press, London, 1998, pp. 95-99.
144. Zoya with Follain, John & Cristofari, Rita, *Zoya's Story,* Harper-Collins Publisher, New York, 2002, p.226.
145. Juan R. I. Cole, "The Taliban, Women, and the Hegelian Private Sphere", in Robert D. Crew and Amin Tarzi (ed), *The Taliban and the Crisis of Afghanistan,* Harvard University Press, London, USA, 2008, p. 118.
146. Barakat, Sultan & Wardell, Gareth, "Capitalizing on Capabilities of Afghan Women: Women's Role in Afghanistan's Reconstruction and Development", *International Labour Organization,* CRISIS Working Paper4,Geneva, 2002, p.9.
147. Yasgur, Batya Świft, *Behind the Burqa,* John Wiley and Sons Publishers, New Jersey, 2002, p.8.
148. Nancy Hatch Dupree, *Afghanistan over a cup of Tea,* Publication by Swedish Committee of Afghanistan based on compilation of essays (and interview) by Nancy Dupree on Afghanistan over the years, Kabul, Afghanistan,2011.
149. Emadi, Hafizulla, *Dynamics of Political Development in Afghanistan: The British, Russian and American Invasions,* Palgrave Macmillan, 2010, p.1.
150. Ibid.
151. Barakat, Sultan & Wardell, Gareth, "Capitalizing on Capabilities of Afghan Women: Women's Role in Afghanistan's Reconstruction and Development", *International Labour Organization,* CRISIS Working Paper4,Geneva, 2002, p.9.
152. Ibid.
153. Emadi, Hafizulla, *Dynamics of Political Development in Afghanistan: The British, Russian and American Invasions,* Palgrave Macmillan, 2010, p.2.
154. Nancy Hatch Dupree, "Women in Afghanistan", *UNIFEM Occasional Paper,* No.9, July 1989.
155. Nancy Hatch Dupree, "Women in Afghanistan", *UNIFEM Occasional Paper,* No.9, July 1989, p.3.
156. Ibid.
157. Ibid, p.3.
158. Ibid, p.3.
159. Ibid.
160. Ibid, p.6.
161. "The Journey to Economic Development", *World Bank Report,* Washington D.C, 1978, cited in "Women in Afghanistan", *UNIFEM Occasional Paper,* No.9, July 1989.
162. Afghanistan Demographic Studies Report, 1975 cited by Nancy Dupree in "Women in Afghanistan", *UNIFEM Occasional Paper,* No.9, July 1989.
163. Nancy Hatch Dupree, "Women in Afghanistan", *UNIFEM Occasional Paper,* No.9, July 1989, p.7.
164. Nancy Hatch Dupree, "Women in Afghanistan", *UNIFEM Occasional Paper,* No.9, July 1989, p.7

165. Ibid.
166. Ibid, p.7.
167. Barakat, Sultan & Wardell, Gareth, "Capitalizing on Capabilities of Afghan Women: Women's Role in Afghanistan's Reconstruction and Development", *International Labour Organization*, CRISIS Working Paper4,Geneva, 2002, p.9.
168. Ibid
169. Wall, J., and Byrd,W., "Brief overview of Afghanistan's economy" *World Bank Report,* 2001.
170. World Bank Global Monitoring Report 2007, Available at: hep://web.worldbank.org/WBSITE/EXTERNAL/EXTDEC/EXTGLOBALMONITOR/EXTGLOMONREP2007/0,,menuPK:3413296~pagePK:64218926~piPK:64218953~theSitePK:3413261,00.html
171. Byravan, S, "Gender and Innova-on in South Asia". 2008(Oeawa: IDRC). Available at: hep://www.idrc.ca/en/ev-- 130670-- 201-- 1-- DO_TOPIC.html.
172. Grace, Jo, " Gender Roles in Agriculture, Case Studis of Five villages in northern Afghanistan", AREU Publication, 2004.
173. Sharecropping out refers to giving land one owns to a farmer to work for a share of the crop. Sharecropping in refers to working on another's land as a farmer for a share of the crop.
174. Grace, Jo, " Gender Roles in Agriculture, Case Studies of Five villages in northern Afghanistan", AREU Publication, 2004, p.6.
175. Coke, A. *Wheat Seed and Agriculture Programming in Afghanistan: Its Potential to Impact on Livelihoods,* Afghanistan Research and Evaluation Unit:, Kabul. 2004.
176. Grace, Jo, " Gender Roles in Agriculture, Case Studies of Five villages in northern Afghanistan", AREU Publication, 2004, p.8.
177. Barakat, Sultan and Gereth Wardell, "Capitalizing on Capacities of Afghan Women", Recovery and Reconstruction Department Paper, Geneva, 2001.
178. Basu Roy, Arpita, " Contemporary Afghanistan, Conflict and Peace-Building", Har-Anand Publishers, 2010, p.74.
179. Saba Gul Khattak, " Refugee Policy Politics: Afghans in Pakistan", *Preliminary Draft Paper,* RCSS, Colombo, 1998.
180. Dupree, N.H. "The Role of the VOLAGs", *Tragedy of Afghanistan* (Bo Huldt and E. Jansson, eds), Croom Helm , London, N.Y, Sydney, 1988.
181. Dupree, Nancy Hatch, "Women in Afghanistan", *UNIFEM Occasional Paper,* No.9, July 1989, p.8.
182. Ibid, p.9.
183. Doubleday, Veronica, "Three Women of Heart", Jonathen Cape, London , 1988.
184. Dupree, Nancy Hatch, "Women in Afghanistan", *UNIFEM Occasional Paper,* No.9, July 1989, p. 10.

185. Skaine, Rosemarie, *The Women of Afghanistan Under the Taliban*, Mc Farland & Company, London,2002.
186. Dupree, Nacy Hatch, " Behind the Veil in Afghanistan",*ASIA*, The Asia Society of New York, New York, 1984.
187. Dupree, Nancy Hatch, "Women in Afghanistan", *UNIFEM Occasional Paper*, No.9, July 1989, p. 10.
188. Ibid.
189. Nancy Hatch Dupree, " The Role of the VOLAGS" in *The Tragedy of Afghanistan*, Bo Huldt and E. Janson, London, 1988.
190. Nancy Hatch Dupree, "Women in Afghanistan", *UNIFEM Occasional Paper*, No.9, July 1989, p.11.
191. Ibid.
192. Arpita Basu Roy, *Contemporary Afghanistan, Conflict and Peace-Building*, Har-Anand Publishers, 2010, p. 39.
193. Arpita Basu Roy, *Afghanistan Towards a Viable State*, Hope India Publication, New Delhi, 2002.
194. *U.S. Department of State Country Report on Human Rights Practices.* Washington, DC: U.S. Department of State; 1998 [Hereafter *Country Report on Human Rights.*].
195. "The Taliban's War on Women", Physicians for Human Rights, United States, 1998. http://www.law.georgetown.edu/rossrights/docs/reports/taliban.pdf
196. Ibid
197. 100 Girls' Schools in Afghan Capital Are Ordered Shut, *The New York Times*, June 17,1998. (Associated Press, June 16, 1998.)
198. "The Taliban's War on Women", Physicians for Human Rights, United States, 1998. http://www.law.georgetown.edu/rossrights/docs/reports/taliban.pdf
199. Griffin, Michael, *Reaping the Whirlwind: The Taliban Movement in Afghanistan*, Pluto Press, London, Sterling and Virginia, 2001, p.142.
200. Sajida, Hayat, " Kabul the city where even the sunrise and sunset have been upset for a long time". An eyewitness report of a RAWA activist from Kabul. Website :www.rawa.org
201. Interview with Bismillah Jan was conducted by the author at Mandawi Bazaar in Kabul, Afghanistan on April5, 2012.
202. Deborah j smith, "Decisions, desires and Diversity: marriage Practices in Afghanistan", AREU Publication, February, 2009,
203. Ibid, p.17.
204. Ibid.
205. Ibid.
206. Sandeep Kumar, *On Edge: The Afghan Passage*, Gyan Publishers, 2011, p 64.
207. Ibid.
208. Interview conducted by the author with the respondent at the Gulbahar Centre of Kabul, Afghanistan. 4th April 2012.

209. Ibid.
210. Sandeep Kumar, Op.cit, P.64.
211. Valentine M. Moghadam, " Revolution, Religion and Gender Politics: Iran and Afghanistan Compared", *Journal of Women's History*, No.4, Winter, 1999, p. 190.
212. Ibid.
213. Ibid, p.170.
214. Hafizullah Emadi, *Politics of Development and Women in Afghanistan*, Paragon House, 1993.
215. Rosemarie,Skaine, *The Women of Afghanistan under the Taliban*, Mc Farland & Company, Inc., Publishers, London, 2000, p.24.
216. Nancy Hatch Dupree, "Afghan Women under the Taliban" in Willam Maly , ed. *Fundamentalism Reborn? Afghanistan and the Taliban*, New York University Press, 1998, pp152-153.
217. Rosemarie,Skaine, *The Women of Afghanistan under the Taliban*, Mc Farland & Company, Inc., Publishers, London, 2000.
218. Cristine Aziz, "Defiance and oppression- the Situation of Women in Afghanistan," Oct 16, 1999. http://essentialfieldguides.weebly.com/
219. Rosemarie,Skaine, *The Women of Afghanistan under the Taliban*, Mc Farland & Company, Inc., Publishers, London, 2000, p.15.
220. Louis Dupree, *Afghanistan*, Princeton University Press, !980, p.446.
221. Hafizullah Emadi, *Dynamics of Political Development in Afghanistan*, Palgrave macmillan, 2010, p.32.
222. Hafizullah Emadi, *Politics of Development and Women in Afghanistan*, Paragon House, 1993.
223. Ibid, 228-229.
224. Christine Aziz, "Defiance and Oppression- the Situation of Women in Afghanistan", *Essential Field Guide to Afghanistan*, 1999. http://www.essentialfieldguides.com/BOOKS/EFG3rdEditionEXCERPT.pdf
225. Moghadam, " Revolution, Religion and Gender Politics: Iran and Afghanistan Compared", *Journal of Women's History*, No.4, Winter, 1999, p.177.
226. Hafizullah Emadi, *Dynamics of Political Development in Afghanistan*, Palgrave macmillan, 2010, p. 65.
227. Hafizullah Emadi, *Dynamics of Political Development in Afghanistan*, Palgrave Macmillan, 2010, p. 65.
228. Moghadam, " Revolution, Religion and Gender Politics: Iran and Afghanistan Compared", *Journal of Women's History*, No.4, Winter, 1999, p. 177.
229. Hafizullah Emadi, *Politics of Development and Women in Afghanistan*, Paragon House, 1993.
230. Rosemarie,Skaine, *The Women of Afghanistan under the Taliban*, Mc Farland & Company, Inc., Publishers, London, 2000, p.15.
231. Louis Dupree, *Afghanistan*, Princeton University Press, 1980.

232. Louis Dupree, *Afghanistan,* Princeton University Press, 1980, 587.
233. Rosemarie Skaine, *The Women of Afghanistan under the Taliban,* Mc Farland & Company, Inc., Publishers, London, 2000, p.15.
234. Ibid, p.17.
235. Hafizullah Emadi, *Politics of Development and Women in Afghanistan,* Paragon House, 1993, p.232.
236. Ibid, pp 232-234.
237. Hafizullah Emadi, *Dynamics of Political Development in Afghanistan,* Palgrave macmillan, 2010, p. 70.
238. Batya Swift Yasgur, *Behind the Burqa,* John Wiley & Sons, Inc. New Jersay, 2002,p. 93.
239. Anthony Arnold, *Afghanistan's Two Party Communism: Parcham Khalq,* Hoover Institute Press, 1983, p.21.
240. Sultan Barakat and Gareth Wardell, "Capitalizing on Capacities of Afghan Women", *Recovery and Reconstruction Department,* Geneva, 2001.
241. Ibid, p.13. (Data cited from Human Rights Watch)
242. Rosemarie Skaine, *The Women of Afghanistan under the Taliban,* Mc Farland & Company, Inc., Publishers, London, 2000, p. 17.
243. Ibid.
244. Dupree, Nancy, "Revolutionary Rhetoric and Afghan Women", *The Asia Scociety,* Occasional Paper, 23, January 1981.
245. Ibid, p.13.
246. Sultan Barakat and Gareth Wardell, "Capitalizing on Capacities of Afghan Women", *Recovery and Reconstruction Department,* Geneva, 2001, *p.13.*
247. Sultan Barakat and Gareth Wardell, "Capitalizing on Capacities of Afghan Women", *Recovery and Reconstruction Department,* Geneva, 2001, *p.13.*
248. Rosemarie Skaine, *The Women of Afghanistan under the Taliban,* Mc Farland & Company, Inc., Publishers, London, 2000, p. 18.
249. Moghadam, " Revolution, Religion and Gender Politics: Iran and Afghanistan Compared", *Journal of Women's History,* No.4, Winter, 1999.
250. Jan Goodwin, *Price of Honour: Muslim Women Lift the Veil of Silence on Islamic World,* Little Brown, Boston, 1994.
251. Sultan Barakat and Gareth Wardell, "Capitalizing on Capacities of Afghan Women", *Recovery and Reconstruction Department,* Geneva, 2001, *p.13.*
252. Rosemarie,Skaine, *The Women of Afghanistan under the Taliban,* Mc Farland & Company, Inc., Publishers, London, 2000, p. 21.
253. Emadi, Op.cit, p.226.
254. Khaled Hosseini, *A Thousand Splendid Suns,* Bloomsbury Publishers, London, 2007, p.159.
255. Khaled Hosseini, *A Thousand Splendid Suns,* Bloomsbury Publishers, London, 2007, p.159.
256. Sultan Barakat and Gareth Wardell, "Capitalizing on Capacities of Afghan Women", *Recovery and Reconstruction Department,* Geneva, 2001, p.14.

257. Hafizullah Emadi, *Dynamics of Political Development in Afghanistan*, Palgrave Macmillan, 2010, pp. 174-175.
258. Ibid
259. Sultan Barakat and Gareth Wardell, Op.cit.
260. Dupree, Louis, *Afghanistan*, Princeton University Press, 1980.
261. Sultan Barakat and Gareth Wardell, "Capitalizing on Capacities of Afghan Women", *Recovery and Reconstruction Department*, Geneva, 2001, p.14.
262. Ibid.
263. Hafizullah Emadi, *Dynamics of Political Development in Afghanistan*, Palgrave Macmillan, 2010, p. 177.
264. Sultan Barakat and Gareth Wardell, "Capitalizing on Capacities of Afghan Women", *Recovery and Reconstruction Department*, Geneva, 2001, p. 15.
265. Eleheh Rostami-Povey, *Afghan Women, Identity and Invasion*, zed Books, London and New York, 2007, p.27.
266. Sultan Barakat and Gareth Wardell, Op.cit.
267. Eleheh Rostami-Povey, *Afghan Women, Identity and Invasion*, zed Books, London and New York, 2007, p.26.
268. Batya Swift Yasgur, *Behind the Burqa*, John Wiley & Sons, Inc. New Jersay, 2002,p.197.
269. Batya Swift Yasgur, *Behind the Burqa*, John Wiley & Sons, Inc. New Jersay, 2002,p.197.
270. Ibid.
271. Ibid.
272. Ibid, p.198.
273. Batya Swift Yasgur, *Behind the Burqa*, John Wiley & Sons, Inc. New Jersay, 2002,p. 208.
274. Sultan Barakat and Gareth Wardell, "Capitalizing on Capacities of Afghan Women", *Recovery and Reconstruction Department*, Geneva, 2001, p. 15.
275. Ibid.
276. Ibid.
277. Ibid, p.16.
278. Batya Swift Yasgur, *Behind the Burqa*, John Wiley & Sons, Inc. New Jersay, 2002,p. 204.
279. Eleheh Rostami-Povey, *Afghan Women, Identity and Invasion*, zed Books, London and New York, 2007, p.27.
280. Eleheh Rostami-Povey, *Ibid.*
281. Sultan Barakat and Gareth Wardell, "Capitalizing on Capacities of Afghan Women", *Recovery and Reconstruction Department*, Geneva, 2001, p. 16.
282. Ibid, P.17.
283. Rosemarie Skaine, *The Women of Afghanistan under the Taliban*, Mc Farland & Company, Inc., Publishers, London, 2000, p. 22.
284. Eleheh Rostami-Povey, Op.cit, p. 38.
285. Rosemarie Skaine, *The Women of Afghanistan under the Taliban*, Mc Farland & Company, Inc., Publishers, London, 2000, p. 61.

286. Revolutionary Association of the Women in Afghanistan, "Some of the Restrictions Imposed by Taliban on Women in Afghanistan," http://www.rawa.org/rules.htm (accessed on 27.07.2012)
287. Rashid, Ahmed, *Descent into Chaos, How the war against Islamic Extremism is being lost in Pakistan, Afghanistan and Central Asia,* Penguin Books, 2008.
288. Emadi, Hafizullah, *Dynamics of Political Development in Afghanistan, the British, Russian and American invasions,* Palgrave Macmillan, 2010.
289. Ibid, p.206.
290. Eleheh Rostami-Povey, *Afghan Women, Identity and Invasion,* zed Books, London and New York, 2007, pp.40-41.
291. Ibid.
292. Pierre Tristam, " President Bush Launches Attack on Afghanistan" (Speech to the Nation by George W. Bush, President of USA on 7th October, 2001), *Middle East Issues,* http://middleeast.about.com/od/afghanistan/qt/me081007b.htm
293. Feinstein, Barry A, "Operation enduring freedom: legal dimensions of an infinitely just Operation"
294. Eleheh Rostami-Povey, *Afghan Women, Identity and Invasion,* zed Books, London and New York, 2007, pp.40-41.
295. Rashid, Ahmed, *Descent into Chaos,* Penguin Books, 2008.
296. Ibid.
297. Ibid.
298. Arpita Basu Roy, *Contemporary Afghanistan,* Har-anand Publication, New Delhi., 2010, pp.152-153.
299. Ann Jones, *Kabul in Winter,* Picador, Metropolitan Book, 2006, p.84.
300. Orzala Ashraf Nemat "Afghan Women: Agents of Peace- Or its Victim?"*A Century Foundation Report,* 2011.p.3.
301. Ann Jones, Op.cit.
302. Masuda Sultan, "Afghan Women on the Agenda for Peace", *Women Waging Peace Policy Commission,* Executive, Summary, 2005, p.4
303. Ibid, p. ix.
304. Ibid, p.6.
305. B. Nussbaum, 'Liberation', *Business Week* 3 December, 200132–3.
306. R. Lacayo, 'The Women of Afghanistan', *Time,* 3 December, 2001, 34–49
307. Ibid, p.36.
308. Ibid, p.85.
309. George Marcus, *BBC News Online,* November 2001 cited in Sultan Barakat and G. Wardell , "Capitalizing on Capacities of Afghan Women", December 2001.
310. "We Have the Promise of the World", *Human Rights Watch,* 2009.
311. United Nations Development Programme (UNDP) Report Afghanistan, 2006. http://www.undp.org.af/publications/KeyDocuments/UNDP%20AF%20ANNUAL%20REPORT%202006.pdf

312. World Bank in Afghanistan, 2007, http://siteresources.worldbank.org/AFGHANISTANEXTN/Resources/305984-1171214014238/AFUpdateApr07.pdf
313. Central Intelligence Agency Factbook, 2005. https://www.cia.gov/news-information/press-releases-statements/press-release-archive-2005/pr04282005.html
314. Eleheh Rostami-Povey, *Afghan Women, Identity and Invasion,* zed Books, London and New York, 2007, p. 43.
315. Masuda Sultan, Women Waging Peace Policy Commission, "Afghan Women on the Agenda for Peace", 2005, Part. One, p.10
316. "Stronger Women stronger Nation", *The Afghanistan Report,*2009, p-12.
317. Kandyioti, Deniz "Old Dilemmas or New Challenges? The Politics of Gender and Reconstruction in Afghanistan," *Development and Change, Vol-38, No-2,* 2007.
318. Orzala Ashraf Nemat "Afghan Women: Agents of Peace- Or its Victim?"*A Century Foundation Report,* 2011.
319. Ibid.
320. Deniz Kandiyoti, "The Politics of Gender and Reconstruction in Afghanistan," Occasional Paper 4, United Nations Research Institute for Social Development, 2005.
321. "Afghan Women's Right on the Brink", *ACTIONAID Report. http://actionaidusa.org/news/pr/On_the_brink_Afghan_womens_rights.pdf*
322. National Action Plan for the Women of Afghanistan (NAPWA): The Government's main vehicle for implementing policies and commitments to advance the status of women 2007-2017, Islamic Republic of Afghanistan. http://sgdatabase.unwomen.org/uploads/National%20Action%20Plan%20for%20the%20Women%20of%20Afghanistan%202007%20to%202017.pdf
323. Kirk Semple, 'Afghan women slowly gaining protection', New York Times, 2 March 2009: http://www.nytimes.
324. United Nations, Women's Indicators and Statistics database (www.ipu.org): http://www.ipu.org/parline-e/ reports/2381_E.htm
325. Anjali Kwatra, A just peace? The legacy of war for the women of Afghanistan, ActionAid, September 2011: http:// www.actionaid.org.uk/doc_lib/a_just_peace.pdf
326. "Afghan Women's Right on the Brink", *ACTIONAID Report. http://actionaidusa.org/news/pr/On_the_brink_Afghan_womens_rights.pdf*
327. Rachel Reid, The 'Ten-Dollar Talib' and Women's Rights, Human Rights Watch, 2010: www.hrw.org/sites/default/ files/reports/afghanistan0710webwcover.pdf
328. Maryam Sakeenah, "Status of Women in Post Taliban Afghanistan" (incomplete)
329. Ibid.
330. This list of women's rights NGOs has been taken from the website www.afghanistan-analyst.org

331. The Bonn Agreement, 2001 http://www.afghanistanembassy.no/afghanistan/government/core-state-documents/bonn-agreement (accessed on 8.8.2012)
332. The London Conference on Afghanistan, 'Afghanistan Compact: Building on Success'. http://www.nato.int/isaf/docu/epub/pdf/afghanistan_compact.pdf (accessed on 18, May. 2012)
333. Afghanistan Online, "Girls Miss Out on Full Education", Kabul, February 2007. www.afghan-web.com
334. Masuda Sultan, "Afghan Women on the Agenda for Peace", *Women Waging Peace Policy Commission*, 2005, p.7.
335. "Afghanistan: Women's Rights", Evaluation Report by the Afghanistan Independent Human Rights Commission (AIHRC), 2007. www.aihrc.org
336. Ibid.
337. Ibid.
338. Maryam Sakeenah, Status of Women in Post Taliban Afghanistan, *TRANSCEND Media Service.* (Incomplete-Year not found)
339. Afghanistan National Development Strategy, 2007. http://www.nps.edu/programs/ccs/Docs/Pubs/unands_Jan.pdf
340. Afghanistan: Women's Rights", Evaluation Report by the Afghanistan Independent Human Rights Commission (AIHRC), 2007. www.aihrc.org
341. Amnesty International Report, "Afghanistan: Women Still Under Attack", AI Index ASA 11/007/2005, www.amnesty.org
342. Ibid.
343. Masuda Sultan, Women Waging Peace Policy Commission, "Afghan Women on the Agenda for Peace", 2005, Part Two, p.20
344. Amnesty International Report, "Afghanistan: Women Still Under Attack", AI Index ASA 11/007/2005, www.amnesty.org
345. Stephen Biddle, Fotini, Christina and Alexander, Their, "Defining success in Afghanistan: What can United States Accept?", *Foreign Affairs*.89, no.4, July-Aug, 2010.
346. "Stronger Women Stronger Nation", Report Series, *Afghanistan Report*, 2009.
347. "Progress for Women Is Progress for All." Fact Sheet, *UN Development Fund for Women (UNIFEM), 2008.*
348. Afghanistan National Development Strategy2008-2013, Executive Summary, http://www.ands.gov.af/ands/final_ands/src/final/ANDS%20Executive%20Summary_eng.pdf.
349. ANDS Gender Equity Cross Cutting Strategy. http://www.ands.gov.af/ands/final_ands/src/final/sector_strategies/Gender%20Strategy%20-%20English.pdf. cited in "Stronger Women Stronger Nation", Report Series, *Afghanistan Report*, 2009.
350. Ibid.
351. "Stronger Women Stronger Nation", Report Series, *Afghanistan Report*, 2009.

352. UNIFEM Afghanistan – Fact Sheet 2008, "Progress for Women Is Progress for All." http://www.unama-afg.org/news/_publications/fact%20 sheets/2008/UNIFEM%20Fact%20Sheet2008%20-%20%20updated.pdf cited in "Stronger Women Stronger Nation", Report Series, *Afghanistan Report*, 2009.
353. Who Answers to Women? Gender and Accountability, Progress of the World's Women 2008/2009. *UNIFEM Report*. http://www.unifem.org/progress/2008/media/POWW08_Report_Full_Text.pdf *citing* Government of Afghanistan, Ministry of Women's Affairs. 2007. "Women and Men in Afghanistan: Baseline Statistics on Gender." Final Draft Endorsed by Central Statistics Office.
354. Women hold 68 out of 249 seats in the Wolesi Jirga and 23 out of 102 seats in the Mesherano Jirga Fact Sheet 2008: "Progress for Women Is Progress for All", *UNIFEM Report*, 2007http://www.iknowpolitics.org/sites/default/files/unifem_factsheet_07.pdf
355. Ibid.
356. "Stronger Women Stronger Nation",Op.cit.
357. Afghanistan: Role of Women in Afghanistan's Future, Ch.4 Work and Employment, World Bank. http://siteresources.worldbank.org/AFGHANISTANEXTN/Resources/AfghanistanGenderReport.pdf
358. Ibid.
359. Ibid.
360. "A better Investment Climate for Everyone", *World Bank Development Report*, 2005. http://siteresources.worldbank.org/INTWDR2005/Resources/complete_report.pdf
361. Interview with Abeda was conducted by the author at the Vocational Training Centre run by SEWA at Bagh-e Zanana in Kabul, Afghanistan on 6th April, 2012.
362. Cheryl, Benard, Seth G. Jones ,"Women and Nation Building", *RAND Centre for Middle East Public Policy*, 2008.p.91.
363. Amnesty International, 2004a.
364. *Gender Disparities as a Challenge to Human Development, Afghanistan National Human Development Report*, United Nations Press, New York, January, 2004a.
365. Interview was conducted by the author with a working Afghan girl at a Research organization in Sher-e-Naw in Kabul, Afghanistan on 4th April, 2012. The respondent shared her view on condition of anonymity.
366. Maryam Sakeenah, Status of Women in Post Taliban Afghanistan, *TRANSCEND Media Service.* (Incomplete-Year not found)
367. Ann Jones, *Kabul in Winter*, Picador, Metropolitan, Henry Holt and Company, New York, 2006.p.108.
368. Interview carried on by the author with a Minister of MOWA in Kabul, Afghanistan who shared her views on condition of anonymity, April5, 2012.
369. Interview with Naheed was conducted by the author in Kabul, Afghanistan on6th April 2012 in APPRO's office at Taimani.

370. British Broadcasting Service, "Afghan Women Suffer Violence", December 26, 2006, www.bbcnews.com
371. Revolutionary Association of the Women of Afghanistan, "No Real Change for Afghan Women", October 31, 2006. www.rawa.org
372. These words were spoken by Mariam Rawi, senior member of the Revolutionary Association of the Women of Afghanistan (RAWA), at a speech she delivered at the University of South Australia on the topic of "Women in Afghanistan Today: Hopes, Achievements and Challenges," on April 27, 2006, cited in Maryam Sakeenah, Status of Women in Post Taliban Afghanistan, *TRANSCEND Media Service*
373. Ibid.
374. Ibid.
375. The Washington Post, November 20, 2005, cited in Maryam Sakeenah, Status of Women in Post Taliban Afghanistan, *TRANSCEND Media Service.*
376. The Communique of the Revolutionary Association of the Women of Afghanistan (RAWA), on the Universal Human Rights Day on December 10, 2007. www.rawa.org
377. "Afghanistan: Humanity Denied", report by Human Rights Watch, 2006. www.hrw.org
378. Ibid.
379. Maryam Sakeenah, Status of Women in Post Taliban Afghanistan, *TRANSCEND Media Service.*
380. British Broadcasting Service, "Afghan Women Suffer Violence", December 26, 2006, www.bbcnews.com
381. Maryam Sakeenah, Op.cit.
382. British Broadcasting Service, "Afghan Women Suffer Violence", December 26, 2006, www.bbcnews.com
383. Maryam Sakeenah, Op.cit.
384. "Afghanistan: Women's Rights", Evaluation Report by the Afghanistan Independent Human Rights Commission (AIHRC), 2007. www.aihrc.org.
385. "Afghanistan: Women's Rights", Evaluation Report by the Afghanistan Independent Human Rights Commission (AIHRC), 2007. www.aihrc.org
386. Amnesty International Report, "Afghanistan: Women Still Under Attack", AI Index ASA 11/007/2005, www.amnesty.org
387. Ibid.
388. British Broadcasting Service, "Afghan Women Suffer Violence", December 26, 2006, www.bbcnews.com
389. Ibid.
390. Amnesty International Report, "Afghanistan: Women Still Under Attack", AI Index ASA 11/007/2005, www.amnesty.org
391. "Afghanistan: Women's Rights", Evaluation Report by the Afghanistan Independent Human Rights Commission (AIHRC), 2007. www.aihrc.org
392. Quoted on the website of the Revolutionary Association of Women in Afghanistan (RAWA). www.rawa.org

393. United Nations News Centre report, "Violence Against Women in Afghanistan remains Dramatic", July 18, 2005, Reproduced by www.rawa.org, cited in Maryam Sakeenah, Status of Women in Post Taliban Afghanistan, *TRANSCEND Media Service.*
394. Ibid.
395. British Broadcasting Service, "Afghan Women Suffer Violence", December 26, 2006, www.bbcnews.com
396. Amnesty International Report, "Afghanistan: Women Still Under Attack", AI Index ASA 11/007/2005, www.amnesty.org
397. Maryam Sakeenah, Status of Women in Post Taliban Afghanistan, *TRANSCEND Media Service.*
398. Ibid.
399. Official statement of the Revolutionary Association of the Women of Afghanistan (RAWA) on the 7th anniversary of the U.S invasion of Afghanistan, "Neither the U.S nor the Taliban_ Long Live the Struggle of Independent and Democratic Forces of Afghanistan", October 7, 2008.
400. Ibid.
401. Maryam Sakeenah, Status of Women in Post Taliban Afghanistan, *TRANSCEND Media Service.*
402. Amnesty International Report, "Afghanistan: Women Still Under Attack", AI Index ASA 11/007/2005, www.amnesty.org
403. Maryam Sakeenah, Ibid.
404. Revolutionary Association of the Women of Afghanistan, "No Real Change for Afghan Women", October 31, 2006. www.rawa.org
405. "Afghanistan: Women's Rights", Evaluation Report by the Afghanistan Independent Human Rights Commission (AIHRC), 2007. www.aihrc.org
406. Amnesty International Report, "Afghanistan: Women Still Under Attack", AI Index ASA 11/007/2005,www.amnesty.org
407. Maryam Sakeenah, Status of Women in Post Taliban Afghanistan, *TRANSCEND Media Service.*
408. United Nations News Centre report, "Violence Against Women in Afghanistan remains Dramatic", July 18, 2005. Reproduced by www.rawa.org
409. Amnesty International Report, "Afghanistan: Women Still Under Attack", AI Index ASA 11/007/2005, www.amnesty.org
410. British Broadcasting Service, "Afghan Women Suffer Violence", December 26, 2006, www.bbcnews.com
411. Afghanistan Online, "Plight of the Afghan Woman", March 2008. www.afghan-web.com
412. Communique of the Revolutionary Association of the Women of Afghanistan (RAWA), International Women's Day, March 8, 2008. www.rawa.org
413. Amnesty International Report, "Afghanistan: Women Still Under Attack", AI Index ASA 11/007/2005, www.amnesty.org

414. Ann Jones, Op.cit, p.137.
415. Ann Jones, *Kabul in Winter,* Picador, Metropolitan, Henry Holt and Company, New York, 2006.p. 109.
416. Discussion with Ana Hozyainoza of APPRO was conducted by the author in her office at Taimani, Kabul, Afghanistan on 5th April 2012.
417. Interview with Marriam Wafa was conducted by the author at APPRO guest House at Taimani in Kabul Afghanistan on 6th April 2012.
418. Interview with Arif was conducted by the author at AFC outlet at Shahr-e Naw in Kabul Afghanistan on 6th April 2012.
419. Rabia Balkhi, See Wikipedia, http://en.wikipedia.org/wiki/Rabia_Balkhi (accessed on 10.8.2012)
420. Nancy Hatch Dupree, "When thinking of Afghan women don't think embroidery, think cop!",*Afghanistan over a Cup of Tea,* Swedish Committee of Afghanistan Publication, 2011.
421. Radha Yodhavir, "Biography: Queen Gawhar Shad of Afghanistan", *Helium,* http://www.helium.com/items/1926370-timurids-queen-gawhar-shad-afghanistan (accessed on 10.8.2012)
422. Nancy Hatch Dupree, "When thinking of Afghan women don't think embroidery, think cop!", Op.cit.
423. Ibid.
424. Nancy Hatch Dupree, "When thinking of Afghan women don't think embroidery, think cop!", Op.cit.
425. Author's interactions with Tariq Sapi took place during her field trip to Afghanistan, as a part of her research for this book between 1-8th April, 2012.
426. Author's interactions with Abdullah Jan took place during her field trip to Afghanistan, as a part of her research for this book between 1-8th April, 2012.
427. Information was gathered by the author from Department of Fine Arts of Kabul University during her field trip to Afghanistan as part of her field trip in April 2012.
428. Information gathered from the brochure of *Centre for Contemporary Art Afghanistan.* (KC:Any other info needed?
429. Ibid.
430. Ibid.
431. Fareeha Ghezal's point of view has been put forward in *Gaahnaam-e-Honar* Magazine, Centre for Contemporary Art Afghanistan, 2010, p.56.
432. Information gathered from the brochure of *Centre for Contemporary Art Afghanistan.* (KC:Any other info needed?
433. Interview of Shahbanoo Sadat was published in "Afghan Youth and United Nations", *United Nation's News Letter on Afghanistan,* Issue 3, 2011, p.3.
434. Ibid.
435. Present in over 800 universities, over 800 universities, in 89 countries and territories, AIESEC, the world's largest student organization, is the international platform for young people to discoverand develop their potential so as to have a positive impact in society. http://www.aiesec.org/cms/aiesec/AI/Asia%20Pacific/AFGHANISTAN/aiesec_afg/

436. "Voices of Youth", *United Nation's News Letter on Afghanistan,* Issue 3, 2011, p.3.
437. Ibid.
438. Ibid.
439. Ibid.
440. Ibid.
441. Quoted in the Factsheet "Women's rights in Afghanistan", President, December 17, 2006. www.fco.gov.uk/en/fco
442. Interview conducted by the author with Master Trainers at the Vocational Training Centre run by SEWA at Bagh-e Zanana,in Kabul, Afghanistan, April, 2012.
443. Spink Jeaniene, "Teachers' Education and Professional Development in Afghanistan". Afghanistan Research and Evaluation Unit (AREU) Publication. Kabul, Afghanistan, 2004.
444. Interview was conducted with personnel's from Afghanistan's Ministry of Education at Serena Hotel, Kabul, Afghanistan, 4th April 2012.
445. Data Provided by Ministry of Education, Afghanistan to the author during the field visit to Kabul in April 2012.
446. Anwesha Ghosh, "India Nurtures Afghanistan's Future: perceptions of Afghan Students in India", *Indian Embassy Kabul Journal-HIND,* April Issue, 2012, P.3.
447. Ibid, .p4.
448. "Voices of Youth", *United Nation's News Letter on Afghanistan,* Op.cit.
449. Ibid.
450. This was told to the Author by one of her FB friends from Afghanistan on condition of anonymity.
451. Mariam, an education girl from Kabul told this to the author during an interview conducted at her house in Sher-e-Naw, Kabul, April 2012.
452. "Voices of Youth", *United Nation's News Letter on Afghanistan,* Op.cit.p.5.
453. Interview conducted by the author with students of Sketeistan at the training centre near Ghazni Statidum and also with Officials at UNAMA in Kabul Afghanistan, April 2012.
454. Ariadna Alvarado, "Young Journalist making her Mark", *Afghan Youth and the United Nations,* Issue 3, 2011,p.7.
455. Ibid
456. "Women Police Officers receive their Diplomas", Dutch Ministry of Foreign Affairs. http://www.minbuza.nl/en/news/2012/01/women-police-officers-in-afghanistan-receive-their-diploma.html (accessed on 12.8.2012)
457. "Building More Capable Afghan Police",*Afghan Youth and the United Nations,* Issue 4, 2011,p.4.
458. Mandy Clark, "Female Afghan Police Officers Face Elevated Risks", *CBS News,* 4th October 2011. http://www.cbsnews.com/2100-500202_162-20115169.html (accessed on 12.8.2012)

459. Nancy Hatch Dupree, "when thinking of Afghan women don't think embroidery, think cop!", Swedish Committe Report on Afghanistan, 2010.
460. Mandy Clark, "Female Afghan Police Officers Face Elevated Risks", *CBS News,* 4th October 2011. http://www.cbsnews.com/2100-500202_162-20115169.html (accessed on 12.8.2012)
461. "Amplifying Afghans' concerns at Bonn", *Afghanistan and United Nations,* Issue 5, 2011, p.2.
462. Ibid.
463. Ibid.
464. Sippi Azarbaijani-Moghaddam, *Women's group in Afghan Civil Society,* Kabul, 2006, pp. 138-139.
465. Kai Ryssdal, "Investing in Female Entrepreneurs in Afghanistan", *Market Place World,* March 11, 2011. http://www.marketplace.org/topics/world/investing-female-entrepreneurs-afghanistan (accessed on 12.8.2012)
466. Juan Jose Guemes Barrois, "Afghan Women are venturing Out", posted on facebook on31 January 2011 at 02:58pm. facebook.com/notes/juan-josé-güemes-barrios/afghan-women-are-venturing-out/10150094413308840
467. Ibid.
468. Stephanie Hearty, "Afghanistan's Supergran Crime buster on Wheels", BBC World Service, 27th May, 2012. *http://www.bbc.co.uk/news/magazine-18145805*
469. Ibid.
470. Stephanie Hearty, "Afghanistan's Supergran Crime buster on Wheels", *BBC World Service,* 27th May, 2012. http://www.bbc.co.uk/news/magazine-18145805
471. "Running in Olympic is like Winning Gold for Afghan Girl", *The Hindu,* August 4, 2012.
472. Ibid.
473. Nancy Hatch Dupree, "when thinking of Afghan women don't think embroidery, think cop!", Swedish Committe Report on Afghanistan, 2010.
474. Interview with the young Afghan girl in her early twenty's, currently in India for her higher studies told this to the author in condition of anonymity in Cuttak, Orissa, 12th June, 2012.
475. Ann Jones, *Kabul in Winter,* Metropolitan Books, Henry Holt and Company, New York, 2006,p.172.
476. Ibid, pp.174-175.
477. Interview with the Afghan women in her late 20s, was carried out by the author in the office of an International NGO in Wazir Akbar Khan on 5th April 2012.
478. "Gender Based Violence: A study of Three Universities in Afghanistan", *Gender Studies Institute, Kabul University* in cooperation with UNESCO and UNDP, March 2010.
479. "Gender Based Violence: A study of Three Universities in Afghanistan", *Gender Studies Institute, Kabul University* in cooperation with UNESCO and UNDP, March 2010.

480. Ibid.
481. Group discussion was conducted with the students of Kabul University at the KU Campus by the author during her field trip to Kabul, Afghanistan from 1-8 April 2012.
482. Ann Jones, *Kabul in Winter,* Metropolitan Books, Henry Holt and Company, New York, 2006,p. 109.
483. Ann Jones, *Kabul in Winter,* Metropolitan Books, Henry Holt and Company, New York, 2006,p.174.
484. Ibid, p.100.
485. Deepali Gaur Singh, "16 year old girl victim of honour killing in Germany", *Kabul press.*May14, 2009. http://kabulpress.org/my/spip.php?article3495
486. Discussion with the respondent was carried out by the author during her field trip to Kabul, Afghanistan from 1-8 April 2012.
487. Ann Jones, *Kabul in Winter,* Metropolitan Books, Henry Holt and Company, New York, 2006.p.175.
488. Graham Bawley, "Wed and tortured at 13, Afghan girl finds Justice", *The New York Times,* August 11, 2012. http://www.ndtv.com/article/world/wed-and-tortured-at-13-afghan-girl-finds-rare-justice-253864
489. Interview Nazia Jan was carried out by the author at a Research organization at Shahr –e-Naw in Kabul, Afghanistan during her field trip to Kabul, Afghanistan from 1-8 April 2012.
490. Ann Jones, *Kabul in Winter,* Metropolitan Books, Henry Holt and Company, New York, 2006.p.176.
491. Ibid.
492. Ibid.
493. Graham Bawley, "Wed and tortured at 13, Afghan girl finds Justice", *The New York Times,* August 11, 2012. http://www.ndtv.com/article/world/wed-and-tortured-at-13-afghan-girl-finds-rare-justice-253864
494. Ibid.
495. Ann Jones, *Kabul in Winter,* Metropolitan Books, Henry Holt and Company, New York, 2006.p.179.
496. Ibid
497. Interviews Shiela nd Massouda were carried out by the author at a Research organization at Shahr –e-Naw in Kabul, Afghanistan during her field trip to Kabul, Afghanistan from 1-8 April 2012.
498. Ibid.
499. Jones, *Kabul in Winter,* Metropolitan Books, Henry Holt and Company, New York, 2006.p. 117.
500. Ann Jones, *Kabul in Winter,* Metropolitan Books, Henry Holt and Company, New York, 2006.p. 117.
501. Orzala Ashraf Nemat , Ibid, p. 26.
502. "Survay of Afghan People",*Asia Foundation Report, 2011. http://asiafoundation.org/country/afghanistan/2011-poll.php (accessed on 18.5.2012).*

503. "Afghanistan Women and Girls Seven Years On", Report by Womankind Worldwide, February 2008. http://www.womankind.org.uk/wp-content/uploads/2011/02/taking-stock-final-proof-14-Feb-08.pdf (accessed on 18.5.2012)
504. "Violence Against Women Primary Database Report", *UN Development Fund for Women* (UNIFEM), March 2008, available at http://www.unhcr.org/refworld/category,COI,UNIFEM,,AFG,4c2af52a2,0.html (accessed 19.5.2012) .
505. Ibid.
506. Interview with Dr. Hafeeza was conducted by the author on 8th April, 2012 at Kabul international Airport, Kabul, Afghanistan at around 10 am.
507. Interview with the respondent was conducted by the author on 5th April, 2012 at AREU Office at Sharh-e-Nau, Kabul,Afghanistan at around 3.p.m.
508. Interviews were conducted by the author with four women working with Roshan Telecommunication Company in Kabul on 6th April, 2012 at their office in Shahr-e-Nau. This was told on condition of anonymity.
509. Group discussion and Interviews were conducted with six female students from University of Kabul by the author on 2nd April 2012 at the Kabul University Campus, Kabul, Afghanistan between 12 to 1 pm.
510. Zahir, Estarabi, "Concerns grow as Afghan Speculate on Post 2014 Realities", *Bamdad.Af,* http://www.bamdad.af/english/story/1736 (accessed on 19.5.2012).
511. Interview with Mr. Janan Mosazai, Spokesperson of Afghanistan Foreign Ministry was conducted by the author on 6th April, 2012 at Taimani, Kabul, Afghanistan at about 6 pm.
512. Interview with Mr. Tariq Sapi was conducted by the author on 3rd and 4th April, 2012 at Kabul City Centre, Kabul, Afghanistan.
513. "Taliban Poison Drinking Water in Afghan School, 150 Girls Hospitalised", INDIA TV, April 18, 2012. http://www.indiatvnews.com/news/world/taliban-poison-drinking-water-in-afghan-school-girls-hospitalized-7512.html
514. "The Human Cost: The Consequence of Insurgent Attacks in Afghanistan", Human Rights Watch, April 15, 2007. http://www.hrw.org/en/reports/2007/04/15/human-cost.
515. Interview with Meena Jan was conducted by the author on 2nd April 2012 at her office in Wazir Akbar Khan in Kabul Afghanistan.
516. Group discussion with the author was carried out with a few Afghan women at a renowned Research organization in Kabul at their office in Shahr-e-Naw in Kabul, Afghanistan 7th April, 2012.
517. Najmuddin A Shaikh, "Taliban Attack in Kabul", *Dawn.com,* April 18, 2012. http://dawn.com/2012/04/18/taliban-attack-in-kabul/
518. Telephonic Interview conducted by the author with the respondent on 20th April 2012 and the respondent expressed her views on condition of anonymity.

519. This was shared to the author by Afghan respondents who were contacted via phone and email to know their responses after the attack after 18th April 2012.
520. Telephonic Interview conducted by the author with the respondent on 20th April 2012 and the respondent expressed her views on condition of anonymity.
521. Interview with Simin Jan was conducted by the author on 2nd April 2012 at her office in Shahr-e-Naw in Kabul Afghanistan.
522. Interview with Marriam Jan was conducted by the author on 7nd April 2012 at Taimani in Kabul Afghanistan.
523. Interview conducted by the author with the respondent on 6th April 2012 at an office in Shahr-e-Naw and the respondent expressed her views on condition of anonymity.
524. "Ministers 'United' on Afghanistan", *BBC News,* May 23, 2010.
525. "Promise, Promise", A Brief Paper for the Kabul Conference on Afghanistan, July 2012. www.oxfam.org
526. "Promise, Promise", A Brief Paper for the Kabul Conference on Afghanistan, July 2012. www.oxfam.org
527. Nancy Hatch Dupree, "When thinking of Afghan Women don't think of Embroidery, think Cop!", *Afghanistan Over a cup of Tea,* Swedish Committee Report, 2010.
528. Ibid.
529. Ibid.

ANNEXURE

Afghan girls going to schools

Afghan woman at a workshop

At Bagh-e-Zanana, Kabul

At Habibia High School, Kabul

At Kabul University

Current state of the Darul Aman Palace in Kabul

Interview with Shahmahmood Miakhel, Country Director, USIPJPG

Local transport carrying women and children

Marketplace in Kabul

Mud dwellings in old Kabul

Pictures of members of Skateistan

Shops selling wedding dresses for women

Women at work in Kabul

Women crossing roads in Kabul